Vic Taylor

*

Reminiscences of a Showman

*

With an Introduction by
DAVID ROBINSON

ALLEN LANE THE PENGUIN PRESS

First published in 1971

Allen Lane The Penguin Press
Vigo Street, London W1

ISBN 0 7139 0267 1

Printed in Great Britain by
W. & J. Mackay & Co. Ltd, Chatham
Set in Monotype Bulmer

Contents

Introduction   vii

Chapter 1   1
My early days; introducing my uncle, a phrenologist; the peep-show; pitching; a gang of crooks; circuses; the meeting with Captain Kettle; I leave school; at Oxford; back to Portsmouth

Chapter 2   13
The Indian Fakirs; the Painless Man; second-sight; further shows with Captain Kettle; 'Zeedah, the Mysterious Hindu Talking Head'; exhibitions cancelled

Chapter 3   22
World War 1914; my father enlists; I repair soldiers' boots; a week with 'Zeedah'; I perform at Dorking, introducing my cousin; I work the lime-light at the Hippodrome; I join the R.N.A.S.

Chapter 4   27
Fort Tregantle; Blandford depot; lifted from Hell to Heaven; Nature's gentleman; I join the Blackbirds Concert Party; drafted to France; cancelled isolation; Scampton Aerodrome; dispersed leave; back to Blandford; Leuchars Aerodrome; North Queensferry; I start cooking

Chapter 5   34
Chef at the Officers' Mess; I organize a concert party; the debating society; I become a hypnotist; I leave North Queensferry; I rejoin my squadron at Gosport; the Punch and Judy Show; I leave the service; illness; a comic catastrophe

Chapter 6   40
My father and I travel on cycles; experience with a gang of crooks; the queer inn; the show at Egham; the Pandeau pipes; an accident; I buy a car; Punch and Judy Shows at schools; Christmas in London; *In the Jungle*; an audition for the music-halls; *Strangers*; Phil Vine

v

Chapter 7   57

Around the halls with the cinematograph; the explosion; the pillory
illusion; booking a band; the band gets inebriated up the Rhondda
Valley; Ben, the blink fencer; back to Oxford; back to Portsmouth

Chapter 8   65

Charlotte Street of former years; I get a drenching; courtship and
marriage

Chapter 9   70

Show work on Selsey Bill; pipes for a lady; a few tricks; Find the
Lady; the banknote trick; the motor accident; trip to Oxford; slight
encounter with a policeman; my father dies

Chapter 10   79

My second meeting with Captain Kettle; the bottler; I carve a set of
Punch and Judy figures; Charlie comes to the fairground; hypnotism
with a coloured man; I lose and find Toby; I join the forces again

Chapter 11   85

I am called up for service; the concert party; my home is bombed at
Portsmouth; my wife goes to Havant; I do shows for Dr Barnardo's
Homes; I help to build Thorney Island theatre; I meet with an old
friend at the Grand Theatre, Brighton; experiences in Northern
Ireland; the I.R.A.; war ends and I get discharged from the R.A.F.

Chapter 12   93

Street shows; a chap named Bunk; cinema club shows; last of a
school show; Punch and Judy; other shows, including meeting with
Earl Jellicoe; on the cinema screen; I take over the pub at Ryde;
Christmas Day, I lose and recover my dress coat and vest; on board
the H.M.S. *Implacable*

Chapter 13   103

Two half-crowns and the inspector; the Ascot Gold Cup; winter
1963 and a journey to Gosport; what happened in the hall; the show
at Southwick; a blunder and success; children's entertainment; a
recollection of old-time performers

Introduction

'At the age of seventy', says Victor Edward White Taylor, 'I have taken a fit in my head, I don't know why, to write my experiences as a showman.' His whole life has the air of a scaled-down Georgian picaresque novel, as he moves from one small adventure to the next, occasionally impelled by fits in his head but more often than not accepting with slight but agreeable surprise what fate offers round the next corner. 'The reader will have noticed', he declares, 'that Providence provided something unusual in my favour, which of course is unexplainable.' Most of his experiences are unintentional – engagements happen through a chance encounter or a bicycle ride to Box Hill rather than by hard hustling – and fleeting. You feel that he prefers it this way, for whenever an engagement is repeated for a year or two, he seems already to be hankering after something else.

The motive force may seem casual, but it has been sufficient to keep him going through seventy years of an eventful life. He started with his father's magic entertainment, suffering as a boy for the sake of art, cramped into a little box as the working parts of 'Zeedah, the Mysterious Talking Hindu Head'. They had occasional rather dubious passages as moving picture showmen, as Punch and Judy men, as publicans. At seventy, with his father long dead, and Vic himself complaining of advancing age, he is still ready enough to do a show or take a fit in his head if the occasion arises.

Evidently it is not really philosophy that has kept him going, or sense of expectation, or even optimism or pessimism to any marked degree. What counts rather is that with a few skills up one's sleeve and a willingness to spot a chance at every turn, one can survive through a kind of obstacle race of rackety vans, electrical explosions, collapsing equipment, confidence tricksters, changes of taste and a couple of wars, emerging with nothing less than a sense of achievement.

This, one supposes, has been the essential equipment of the strolling player and itinerant entertainer since the start of time. For Vic Taylor could have existed in the seventeenth century; certainly he might well be speaking to us from the nineteenth. I doubt though if a Vic Taylor will exist in the twenty-first century. Twenty years ago there were reckoned to be a hundred Punch and Judy Shows in England and Wales; by now the number must have dwindled seriously. And throughout Vic's memoirs, albeit unintentionally, there is a sense of the end of the line. Sites that were there for years are suddenly available no more. Where long queues of children once chanted 'We want Punch and Judy', for 'some reason or other' the demand faded out. At the infants' school where children had enjoyed Vic's entertainment for years, the 'arrangements' are changed and money is no longer available for his fee. Of course it must always have been so in the showman's life; but in the days of those old charlatans he recalls from long ago, in Charlotte Street, Portsmouth, and the old-time performers he describes in his final chapter, there seemed more certainty that for every door that closed another would open.

In Vic's memories, the actual shows and the *mise-en-scène* of Punch and Judy take a distinctly secondary role to all the business of travelling, and lodgings and arranging and being paid. Perhaps this too was always so; for in its origins the Punch and Judy Show was a make-shift affair. The present form of the show, after all, only came into being about 1800, when economic circumstances had killed the travelling marionette shows. The whole marvel of Punch and Judy is the way it found its form under practical and economic pressures which limited the knockabout play to a maximum of two characters on stage at any one time, and so dictated the need for fast and funny dialogue, violent action and clearly defined familiar characters. The troupe was built up through the nineteenth century: Joey the clown was a tribute to Grimaldi, and the negro to T.D.Rice's Jim Crow. By the time that Vic Taylor came to the show, its form was rigidly set (though he tells us that old showmen were unwilling to pass on their secrets or their business); and it is clear that it is all much too familiar to him even for him to be able to describe it – just as most people could only with difficulty give a concrete description of their own mothers.

Vic has a charming and easy and wholly individual literary style, which is a mixture of old showman's parlance, memories of Victorian autobiographies and plain unvarnished chatter. He has an instinct for incident and character and colour. The documentary value of ninety per cent of his stories is slight but he makes them interesting simply by his own delight in them. The woman who bellows out of a doorway has not much point in the narrative except to give a touch of Rowlandson-like colour to one of Vic's perennial adventures with a conked-out van.

He has a light, unemphatic way of sketching a character: the little old woman in red drawers who released herself from a strait-jacket for a living and 'spoke in a very common manner'; the outrageous uncle who declared irrelevantly when the police tried to move him along: 'I stand or fall by Their Majesties the King and Queen, God bless them, I salute them' and later worked himself a spring mattress, when they took him to jail, by a perfectly mendacious story of a bad heart; the old acquaintance who explained his newly acquired proficiency in music with a flourish as if of logic: 'I got a job in the dockyard during the war; and I learnt to play the accordion properly.' For them, like Vic, the oddity of life is the source of its energy.

DAVID ROBINSON

Chapter 1

My early days; introducing my uncle, a phrenologist; the peep-show; pitching; a gang of crooks; circuses; the meeting with Captain Kettle; I leave school; at Oxford; back to Portsmouth

May I say I was born at Oxford in the year 1900, and named Victor Edward White Taylor.

At the age of seventy, I have taken a fit in my head, I don't know why, to write my experiences as a showman.

My father was a magician, and I followed in his footsteps; so when the time came for me to know some of the ways of the world, my father religiously started me on the road to become a magician. I practised and practised manipulation of the hands, such as manipulation of the fingers and palming a coin, until I became proficient enough to make a coin disappear by passing it from one hand to the other. Eventually I was able to palm a few coins. Palming means holding a coin, or coins, by contraction of the muscles towards the wrist in such a manner as though it contains or appears to contain nothing. Having accomplished this, at the age of eight years old, I was able to do a few simple tricks.

My parents being professionals, I travelled with them, so I was unable to attend school regularly; but they did

[1]

not neglect my education, and taught me the rudiments of education. Eventually my parents came to Portsmouth and established a home. I had an aunt and uncle already living there, and I was placed in their care whilst my parents travelled the music-halls.

At the age of eight years old, I attended school regularly and, thanks to my parents' teaching, I was no dunce. During my summer holidays, I was labelled like a bit of luggage and put in charge of the guard, and sent to wherever my parents were performing. I enjoyed the train journey immensely, the guard supplied me with chocolate and ice-cream and, if I had to change trains during the journey, he put me in charge of the next guard, who treated me in like manner. Arriving at my destination, my parents met me at the station, and I travelled with them, having a good time for the remainder of my school holiday. I became very keen on my magic, so much so that I would get up during the night (being a sleep-walker) and perform my tricks, my parents watching to see no harm came to me, and return to bed. Next morning, of course, I knew nothing of what took place; eventually I grew out of this sleep-walking.

I must now bring my uncle, perhaps uncle-in-law, into the picture, he having married my father's sister. He came from a good family but, owing to some trouble, which I will not go into, disgraced the family. However, he was highly intelligent and a well-read man, but eccentric in many ways. His trade was a high-class hand-sewn shoe-maker; apart from this he studied phrenology – a science by which a man's character can be read according to the shape of his head, otherwise known as a bump feeler. I recollect once being in a public bar with him and he was explaining the science of phrenology and, pointing to a man who had rather a big nose, he said: 'This man has a big nose denoting foresight and tact', but the fellow resented this and said: 'And you'll have a big nose if you don't shut yer gob up about me.'

Another time, dressed in silk top hat and frock coat, he placed a banner with pictures of their majesties, King Edward VII and Queen Alexandra, on Southsea beach and, standing by this, started to lecture on phrenology, but soon a policeman came along and asked him if he had a permit for a stand. He had not, and was told to pack up. However, he refused to budge saying: 'I stand or fall by Their Majesties the King and Queen, God bless them, I salute them', and I knew for a fact that actually he was anti-royalist, whereon he was run in; but saying he could not walk far, a taxi was supplied to take him to the police station, and his banner was collected by my much worried aunt. He was fined five shillings for obstruction, or a week's imprisonment. Choosing a week in prison, he remarked that he had never been in prison before, and it would be a novel experience for him. On the second night of imprisonment, he complained about the bed being very hard, which was a bad thing for his heart. As far as I knew, there was nothing wrong with his heart, but it did the trick, and a spring mattress was supplied. On his release, he had to interview the governor of the prison. The governor offered the usual advice, and hoped that he would not get into any trouble again, whereon my

[3]

uncle offered to read the governor's head; whether this was accepted or not I do not know.

Returning to my school-days, I became the marble king, a game played to a great extent in those days. I made a marble contrivance, by procuring a chocolate box; the lid I cut to fix about half an inch from the top, with a groove and a bit of a woman's steel stay busk slotted into the groove, and then I bored some round holes in the top, with five or six rivets around them, and marked them win three, win two, win one. The marble was placed in front of the piece of steel which, when snapped back by the finger, sent the marble whirling around the box; if it did not enter one of the holes the player would lose. The chances of winning were limited owing to the fact that I had purposely tilted the top part of the box to one side; this was so slight that it was unnoticeable, and usually the marble rolled around the box without entering any of the holes. By now, I was a fair conjurer, and used to puzzle the youngsters with tricks that my father had taught me. I was keen on school sports, and was considered a favourite to win the gold watch in swimming, but I met with a motor accident and was laid up for a few weeks, so the contest took place and I lost the chance of winning the gold watch.

My uncle taught my father the trade of shoemaking long before I came into existence, and a very fine shoemaker he was; and when there was a slump in the show line, he would get a seat of work as a journeyman shoemaker; this meant he would be taken on by a shoeshop, the material provided and he would make the boots and shoes at home. During one of these sessions, my father purchased me a model theatre; now I was very keen on theatres, and he made me some marionette figures. My father was as much interested in this theatre as I was, and eventually wrote a play for it, called *Lancashire Lass*, and in the play a ghost was made to appear in a coalmine scene. This was accomplished by having a bit of black gauze stretched across the stage, behind which was a figure representing a ghost. Whilst the light was in front of the gauze nothing was seen, but when this light was turned down and one turned on behind the gauze, the apparition would appear. I fixed the theatre up in my mother's front room and charged the kids a halfpenny admittance to see the show. So successful was this that I contrived to do a show every week during the winter months. After this my father bought me a cinematograph projector; this worked a bit of film in a continuous circle of two boxers, but my father was not satisfied with this; not only did he provide it with acetylene lighting, but converted it with large spools to take two or three hundred-foot lengths of film. Moving pictures was then in its infancy, but some old films could be procured of a race-meeting or football match from some of the junk shops in Portsmouth.

Now, he decided to make a large peep show, and once he had a bee in his bonnet he would carry it out to the letter. Having constructed a box about eight feet long by three feet in width, he stood it on four legs, and inserted the screen in the middle of the box, on which the pictures were to be shown; spy-holes were inserted on projecting parts on the slant, to enable people to view the pictures from both sides of the screen. On one end a sort of a tent was attached, housing the projector. During one of my summer holidays from school, the annual fair came to

Portsdown Hill, Cosham, and my father decided to try out the peep show there; I was to wind the film through and, boy-like, I was eager to take part in the show, so it was placed on a truck and, accompanied by my uncle, I pushed the truck just over four miles to the fair. It was decided to charge twopence to view the pictures, and for my uncle to stand by the show and, after the customers had finished viewing the film, to press them to have their heads read, in other words to have their bumps felt, and their characteristics described accordingly at a nominal fee. It all sounded all right, but it was doomed to dismal failure. Everything was all right for a while, but when some lads tried to have a free look my father gave them a whack across the behind with a stick, and this started the trouble. Others joined in, and during the mêlée, the show collapsed, with me underneath it; fortunately the acetylene light was put out, and the risk of fire avoided. After I was released from the tangled mass, what was left of the show was packed on the truck and, after some refreshment at a pub and the long walk home, the three of us arrived footsore and weary and retired for the night.

Henley regatta came along, and my father never missed going there. He hired a man to punt him along the river at a pound a day; this indeed was money and the chap was invariably the same one every year; it meant a small fortune to him. At various places my father performed his conjuring to the people on the bank and, by means of a bag attached to a long pole, collected the money. This lasted a week, and by that time my father made a considerably large sum of money. For the time being the stage was abandoned and he found that pitching – that is, performing out of doors – was more remunerative.

Until the 1914 war life was fairly pleasant. During a cycle of good summers, droves of visitors from various parts of the country came to Southsea, and I have known the promenade packed with people as early as six o'clock in the morning, while the old paddle steamers took crowds over to the Isle of Wight. Fares were cheap, excursions from London five shillings return by train, which was the only means of transport at the time, and one and six return to the Isle of Wight. Money seemed plentiful, sovereigns and half-sovereigns were spent freely, the country being on the gold standard in those years, and there was plenty to spend it on; all along the beach were vendors with large baskets of fancy hats, swishes, fancy sunshades and suchlike, quick photographers, known as mug fakirs, buskers and performers. Beer was twopence a pint and cigarettes five for a penny. True, wages were low, but the money was of much more value. Income tax was sixpence in the pound, and you had to be extraordinary well off to pay it. People saved for a holiday and they went full out to enjoy themselves. Portsmouth was an exceedingly cheap place to live in and prosperous; I never really saw any dire poverty there, but like any other place of size it had its slummy quarter. The cost of living was low, it had to be, to suit the people's pockets then – there were no fridges and meat, fish and vegetables were at the end of the day sold at give-away prices. People of today have heard about the soup kitchen, what a terrible thing it was, but believe me, I and many more, not really poor, often used to visit the soup kitchen and procured a jug of soup for three-halfpence a quart, and damned good food it was. One of the greatest evils of all was the Workhouse; tramps of all description spent a night or two there, before resuming their travels; and old people, without any means of support – for there was no security then – spent the rest of their lives there, under the most miserable conditions. Thank God, progress has removed such places.

Responsible for the prosperity of Portsmouth was the huge Navy and Army stationed there, likewise the Dockyard; pubs and theatres did a roaring trade apart from outdoor functions; that was the only form of amusement. I often went to the theatre, especially when there was a big illusionist billed, for it was my ambition to become one. Before going in the theatre, standing in the queue, buskers, performers of all types would do their stuff, and collect money. Throughout the year, circuses came to Portsmouth, and built the big top on the common, the largest of these was Lord John Sangers'. A gigantic show and, to advertise it, a parade took place; this was a very colourful event, preceded by clowns playing all sorts of antics, performers on usually white horses, lastly the elephants and wild animals drawn by drays (large flat horse-drawn conveyances). One may wonder how the name of Lord John Sangers came about. It so happened that Colonel 'Buffalo Bill' Cody came to this country from America, with his Wild West Show. There was much rivalry between the two shows and John Sangers, as he was then known, had an idea: if Cody could adopt the title of Colonel Cody, he would go one better and called himself Lord John Sangers. Unfortunately he was murdered by a madman in 1911.

Going about the country at this time was a gang of crooks; they operated under the cloak of advertising agents for bogus firms. They were a villainous lot of the worst order and often seen on the race course; the bookies were terrified of them and their protection racket, for if a bookie did not pay up he was beaten up by their thugs, and his joint wrecked. Known as run-out workers, they provided themselves with cheap swag (goods), and worked from a motor-car; giving away a few pencils, they went on to the larger stuff. When a crowd was assembled, two or three articles were put together, and offered, at, say, half a crown; the purchaser handed the money up, but did not receive the goods right away; a few more goods were placed on top, and a larger sum of money asked for them. The purchaser, thinking it was a bargain, duly handed the money up, and so this went on until no more money could be extracted from the would-be buyer. The purchaser was purposely forgotten and another lot was offered to someone else. Getting tired of waiting for the goods the purchaser might demand his money back or the goods; usually the goods were handed over, and the purchaser found it to be a lot of trash. At one place where my father came in contact with them, they in some way or another upset him, and my father publicly denounced them as a fraud. This infuriated them, and my father had to run for his life; fortunately there was a train just on the move, which he boarded, and more fortunate still it was destined for Portsmouth, otherwise I dare not think of the consequences. Eventually the police got busy and broke this gang up.

From the foregoing, you can gather that my young life was crowded with events. I had turned twelve years of age, and could present a really good conjuring show. Now, there came to Portsmouth a gentleman known as Captain Kettle, a title adopted from the exploits of

Captain Kettle, then running in Pearson's Magazine. He was a very clever illusionist and magician, and opened a show shop in the arcade, off Commercial Road, since demolished. Soon, my father and I became known to him, a short man, with pointed beard and moustache, and almost black eyes; indeed, he looked the part. I was greatly interested, as I was out to further my knowledge of magic. He worked two illusions inside the shop; the human spider, a girl's head resting on a sort of web, inside a cabinet, and that was all that could be seen of her; and La-Maut, where a person entered an upright coffin, and slowly turned into a skeleton, and back again. By arrangement with my father, I took part in another illusion, on the week-end or when school holidays took place. This illusion was on a table: only half a body could be seen, all round and underneath was space, but the ingenious Captain Kettle put all sorts of wheels, springs and suchlike, which didn't mean a thing, under the table. The idea was that I, made up as an Indian, was supposed to be an automaton, and took the money at the door, admission to witness the show inside. I practised keeping very still, and eventually didn't bat an eyelid. On one particular occasion, in front of some people, a woman came up to me and pushed her finger in my cheek, and exclaimed: 'He's alive!' Whereon Captain Kettle whispered in convincing solemn tone, 'Yes, Madam, the living dead.' With this she fled as though a host of demons were behind her.

I was nearly thirteen years of age, and my father insisted that, when thirteen, I should leave school. This came round and, under the pretext of taking me away from Portsmouth, permission was given for me to leave. Before I went, I arranged with the headmaster to give a magical show to the pupils. He readily agreed and the show was a great success. The headmaster was very pleased and said, 'Taylor, you are a credit to this school.' With this compliment, I took my departure.

My father and I went to Oxford for a little while, and found that my Uncle Leonard had entered a competition at the old Empire Theatre, Cowley Road, Oxford, which he won with the comic song, 'Where did you get that hat?' The first prize was most unusual, being a live donkey. Not knowing where to park the animal, they took it to my grandmother's house where my father and I were staying, and tied it up to the mangle in the scullery. During the night, the donkey pulled the mangle all over the place, making a fearful noise. My grandmother, thinking someone had broken into the house, called out to my father; knowing what had happened, I got up immediately and, to my grandmother's amazement, found the donkey harnessed to the mangle. My grandmother immediately exclaimed: 'Get that animal out of here.' My father managed to get it out and tie the donkey to a post in the garden. Next morning my Uncle Leonard and my father found that the animal was alive with vermin, whereon they smothered it with Keating's Powder; not knowing what to do with it, it was eventually sold to a farmer for ten shillings; back at Portsmouth once more, further show business took place with Captain Kettle.

Chapter 2

The Indian Fakirs; the Painless Man; second-sight; further shows with Captain Kettle; 'Zeedah, the Mysterious Hindu Talking Head'; exhibitions cancelled

After leaving school, Captain Kettle formed the 'Indian Fakirs', that was my father, myself, and another fellow called Leslie, and occasionally my mother made up as an Indian woman. It was at the Trades Exhibition, held in the Connaught Drill Hall, Stanhope Road, that Captain Kettle had a side-show, with the Indian Fakirs. The make-up was excellent, except that my father had large blue eyes; but strangely this went unnoticed. To all intents and purposes, the Captain brought the Indian Fakirs to England, from the Punjab, India. I was the Indian boy of this so-called tribe; my knowledge of Indian dialect was limited to two words, 'Salaam Sali', which was frequently done, by bowing and hands touching the forehead, mixed up with back slang, and as many unintelligible sounds as possible, accompanied by much gesticulation.

I was standing with my father and Leslie at the entrance of the show when an elderly chap with a large moustache, attired in check cap, plus-fours, jacket and brown shoes, made straight for the show. As young as I was, I quickly formed the opinion that he was some old colonel that had done some time in India, and this proved to be correct. He jabbered away in some Indian lingo, and all that could be done was salaam sabbing, then my father and Leslie quietly disappeared inside the show, leaving him to me. I must have gone all colours of the rainbow under the grease paint, but just then the Captain came to my aid saying to the old colonel, 'It is very unfortunate for this poor Indian, he is dumb.' Then the old colonel left with a sarcastic grin on his face.

Leslie was known as the Painless Man and the Captain was supposed to hypnotize him. Leslie could roll his eyes until just the white of the eye was seen and raise his arms for an indefinite time. In this position the Captain would light a cigar and plunge it on his arm. This was a very unpleasant sight – you could hear the skin sizzle – but Leslie never flinched. At the end of the magical performance, Leslie was secured to a cross, by handcuffs, steel neck and waist bands and lastly ankle irons. A large sack was placed over him, but in a matter of seconds he released himself. On one occasion, in securing Leslie to the cross, my father nipped a large lump of flesh from his ankle and it bled profusely. After his escape my father was full of apologies to him, but all Leslie said was, 'That's all right, Ted, am I not the Painless Man.' The exhibition over, off came the grease paint, and the Indian Fakirs were no more.

For some time, my father and I practised second-sight or thought reading. This meant that, whilst thoroughly blindfolded, I would describe any article or any number

[14]

on any note handed up by members of the audience. Having accomplished this, my father decked me out with mortar-board cap and Eton suit and described me as the youngest thought reader in the world; whether this was so didn't matter, just a showman's privilege. To achieve this a system of codes were used, which had to be thoroughly memorized. My father went amongst the audience, selected the various articles handed up and passed me the code words for any particular article to be described. If an article was handed up and there was no code word in our system for it, my father simply ignored that article.

The summer of 1913 was glorious weather. Cockles, whelks and tea-stalls, vendors, buskers with their boaters, blazers and cream slacks on, all got down to good business. My father and I pitched at various places over the Isle of Wight and the second-sight act went well. My father insisted on a silver collection only; everything was in full swing; little did people realize that Britain would be at war with Germany in the following year.

In the following autumn my father started to construct an illusion called 'Zeedah, the Mysterious Hindu Talking Head', which I will describe later. A trades exhibition again took place in the Connaught Drill Hall; Captain Kettle had another side-show, presenting two illusions, the 'Human Butterfly', similar to the 'Human Spider', already described, and an illusion called 'The Sphinx'. As my father was engaged elsewhere, I was employed to work the 'Sphinx'.

Made up as an ancient Egyptian, all that could be seen

of me was my head in a box. The Captain would display the box outside the show, saying it contained the head of 'Sphinx'. When sufficient people assembled inside the show, having seen the 'Human Butterfly', the box was placed on a table, and the Captain would say, 'I now introduce to you, "Sphinx"' ', whereon a flap was lowered on the box, revealing my head. When he made some passes in front of my face, I slowly opened my eyes, and the Captain would say, ' "Sphinx" is now awake', after which he would ask me some questions. For a boy I had a fairly low voice, and I answered in a mysterious, deep wavering tone.

The questions ran like this:

'You are from some place beyond our knowledge, "Sphinx".'

'I come from Eternity far beyond the catacombs and pyramids of Egypt.'

'How old are you, "Sphinx"?'

To this question I would reply any fantastic number of years.

'What do you live on, "Sphinx"?'

'I live on sand.'

A few more questions, then the Captain would say:

'You are ready to leave us now, "Sphinx"?', whereon he made a few passes with hands in front of my face. I slowly closed my eyes, the flap of the box was closed and all was ready for the next show. After a while, for some reason or the other, Captain Kettle left Portsmouth, and I never came in contact again with him for a good number of years.

Christmas, 1913, came along, and my father had booked a number of children's shows in which I assisted him. I remember my father having a set of Chinese Linking Rings made for me, they were about ten inches in diameter and nickel plated. When presented they linked and unlinked mysteriously. How proud I was of them, this trick became one of my pet items, and to this very day I have performed 'The Chinese Linking Rings'.

My father had now completed the illusion of 'Zeedah, the Mysterious Hindu Talking Head', and I shall have to let readers into the secret of this illusion, otherwise a proper understanding of what followed would be somewhat vague. To begin with, it was a flat top, about two inches wide, supported by the back part of the same width and a base or box about nine inches in depth, in other words like the letter 'U' turned in a horizontal position. The base was on legs and castors about one foot from the ground. The measurement of the whole thing was about three feet long by two feet wide. The front was supported by two slender battens, about one and a half inches square. On the centre was an assortment of electrical apparatus, which was for show only; at the back were some organ pipes, which were nothing more or less than broom sticks painted in silver, with black apertures cut in them. Dead in the back centre were two much larger organ pipes, hollow, made of tin, painted to represent the same. In the centre of the top a dummy head made up as a Hindu, with speaking tube, and cords attached to turn it from side to side. In front of the base were two drawers, these were dummy ones. Now for the main secret: the whole of the front swung away on hinges, just leaving the back and base, in which I lay on my back, with my legs in an upright or vertical position. The front was swung back, my legs entered the two large organ pipes and the contrivance became one piece again. I was inside and a complete prisoner, so to speak.

It is difficult to explain this illusion, but readers will have the main idea – that I was inside this contrivance. I had a cord attached to the movable mouthpiece of the dummy head, which I controlled to answer questions put by the audience. I could not remain too long in the position that I was, otherwise my legs would become numbed; but after some rehearsals, I found that I could remain inside the contrivance about ten minutes and no longer. The whole idea was that the head was solely controlled by electricity, and by this means, questions and articles handed up by members of the audience would be fully described by the 'Hindu Talking Head'. As my father and I were expert in second-sight this presented no difficulty, and after some rehearsing it was ready to go on the stage.

One thing stands out in my memory: an audition was arranged and after a few tricks my father presented 'Zeedah'. After the show my father was invited to the bar by the agent and manager to discuss business, completely forgetting to release me from the contrivance. My legs were so numbed that in desperation I banged on the sides of the box, and shouted for help. A stage hand happened to be near; on hearing my cries, he was puzzled to know where they came from, although he was quite near the illusion. He got scared and quickly went to the bar say-ing, 'There's something funny going on on the stage.' They all came to the stage and to their amazement I was released; they having no idea that a person could possibly be concealed in such a manner. My legs were so numbed that I collapsed on the stage, but I soon got back to nor-mal.

The result was a run on the music-halls down the West Country. The act went very well. I stood in the wings in tights, during the preliminary of my father's magic, and ready to enter 'Zeedah', which was pushed on the stage. Members of the audience were invited on the stage to inspect the contrivance. After some remarks by my father that 'this invention has revolutionarized electrical science', the performance proceeded; the head answered questions, described various articles handed up by the audience. Of course, the speaking voice was mine through the speak-ing tube.

Finishing the run on the music-halls, a series of trades exhibitions were booked; the first one was at the Town Hall, Stroud, Gloucestershire. Arriving at Stroud with 'Zeedah', my father and I opened there on a Monday; a week had nearly passed, but the whole thing was a flop; the other exhibitions were cancelled, leaving my father and me stranded. However, my father became very friendly with the landlord of the local pub, having shown the customers tricks and entertained them in general. On hearing that the exhibitions had suddenly terminated, the landlord said, 'I have a friend who keeps a hotel at Sharp-ness Point, give him this card and he will arrange an entertainment, I think it will be worth going there.' Taking a chance on this, 'Zeedah' was cloaked at the railway station, and my father and I proceeded on the journey.

Arriving at Sharpness Point, which is situated on the southern side of the Severn Tunnel, it was quite different to what was expected, being a number of docks, railway lines and about a dozen houses; my father and I felt like taking the next train back and going on to Portsmouth; however, on arriving at the hotel the card of the late landlord was presented to the proprietor, and he exclaimed: 'Ah! from my old friend at Stroud, but you have come at a quiet time, there are not many ships in, but come back later, and I will arrange something.'

Meanwhile, arrangements to stay the night had to be made; a hostel was found; on inquiring if a couple of beds could be booked, the chap in charge said, 'Only men working on the ships or docks have these beds.' However, after pleading with him he kindly let my father and me have two, but said, 'You can only stay this one night.' In fact, that was all that was wanted, but going back to the hotel, it was nearly full of captains, mates and anybody connected with ships. The landlord arranged for an entertainment to take place. My father did the conjuring, and I did the second-sight. A collection was made and this was beyond all expectation; the chappie from the hostel was there and he agreed that my father and I could stay at the hostel for as long as was necessary. There were two more hotels there, both proved to pay well for entertainment and, instead of staying one night, three weeks went by before it was decided to return to Portsmouth.

[20]

They gave my father and me a good send-off, and the landlord of the hotel gave us a handsome farewell gift. Calling at Stroud, a stop to thank the landlord of the local there, we picked up 'Zeedah' and so proceeded back to Portsmouth.

Chapter 3

*World War 1914; my father enlists; I repair soldiers'
boots; a week with 'Zeedah'; I perform at Dorking, introducing my cousin; I work the lime-light at the Hippodrome; I join the R.N.A.S.*

I had turned fourteen years of age, and was as ambitious
as ever to become a big illusionist; but under the circumstances that followed this was not to be.

The year 1914 promised to be a good season; the
weather was fine, but owing to disturbances in Europe,
war clouds were gathering. A general mobilization was
called and Germany invaded Holland and Belgium and,
on 4 August 1914, this country declared war on Germany.

The French and British repulsed the German advance
on Paris, with great losses on both sides, and established
the Western front of trench-warfare. People at home
settled down to the conditions of war for four long weary
years.

After a while my father enlisted in the Royal Engineers
and for a time I took a job with a leather merchant.
Finishing with this, I fixed up a workshop in the back
yard and repaired soldiers' boots, having learnt the trade
or most of it whenever my father had cause to work at

shoemaking. Most of the work came from the soldiers stationed at the forts on Portsdown Hill.

At times I was exceptionally busy and then there were times when I was slack; it was all according to how the work came in. My father was stationed in one of the forts near Fareham, Hampshire, and by arrangement with the Commanding Officer and the manager of Fareham cinema, my father put on a show there for a week. 'Zeedah' was the prominent feature on the programme, and you can guess that all the soldiers attended the performance. There was much speculation as to how 'Zeedah' was accomplished, the general theory being that some sort of a gramophone record was employed, and it was impossible to think of any human agency being concealed therein. This belief was so strong that my father arranged to be shut out of the cinema hall during the performance of 'Zeedah'; this was done and the head of 'Zeedah' ceased to talk, and so the mystery, to my knowledge, remained unsolved.

After this event my father was drafted to France; my mother was naturally upset, like most women with their husbands leaving them perhaps never to return. Being the only son, my mother idolized me, and although my father was strict with me I must say that I had the finest parents in the world. Throughout the autumn and the winter I still worked at shoemaking, and my mother was pleased to have me home to keep her company. The summer of 1915 was glorious weather, and I cycled to see my aunt at Dorking, Surrey, who was very fond of me, and treated me as if I was her own son.

I was struck with the peacefulness of Dorking; people went about their business as though a war never existed. There was a space of ground known as the rotunda there, and during one of my slack periods in shoemaking, I applied to the local authority to perform on this space of ground. They consented to this, and I placed a notice there, to the effect that a magical performance would take place at a certain time. Although only fifteen years of age, my previous experience had made a first-class showman of me. At Dorking I had a cousin, Frank Taylor by name. Frank and I were great friends, so much so that he took part in anything that I did in the show line. He was a dapper fellow with a charming personality and similar temperament as myself. At the allotted time for the performance Frank and I were at the rotunda. I fixed up my conjuring table, and laid out my magical props. A few people had gathered there, and after a bit of by-play with cards, a crowd assembled. My cousin bottled for me (the show word for collecting). The collection was very satisfying and was shared out between my cousin and myself fifty-fifty.

After a week-end at Dorking I cycled back to Portsmouth to see if any shoemaking had arrived during my absence. I accomplished the work that came in, and made up some small card tricks, which I intended to sell at the end of my performances. It was mostly on week-ends that I visited Dorking, and I found that my performances were very successful and I sold out of the card tricks. One place my cousin and I did very well at was Redhill, not far from Dorking. On one Bank Holiday Frank and I decided to pay a visit to Box Hill. He had a cycle as well as myself. I strapped my box of tricks on the back and proceeded to Box Hill. Arriving there, Frank and I climbed the hill with our cycles, but hardly saw anyone there. Towards the top I saw some trees, and amongst the trees to my surprise came across a restaurant, full of people, laid out in Continental style. My cousin and I had some refreshment, then I asked the proprietor if I could present a conjuring entertainment to his customers. He gave me permission to do so. At the end of the performance Frank went round with the bag and the collection was colossal; so much so, that it was emptied into a hat, and another one made.

Arriving back at Dorking – the front door was usually open in fine weather – Frank and I rushed in and emptied the money on the table, and proceeded to count it. I casually looked round and remarked, 'Aunt has been busy moving the furniture around.' Then suddenly a woman screamed and, on looking around, I discovered that Frank and I were in the wrong house; it should have been the one next door. The woman knew me and on explaining the mistake it all ended in a good laugh.

I went back to Portsmouth, and as I mentioned before that I could be busy or slack in boot-repairing I paid one or two more visits to Dorking. But people were feeling the pinch of war. It wasn't going too well. The German U-boats were sinking British supply ships in great numbers. There was a general food shortage, and it became worse as the War went on. There was nothing else for me to do but to repair soldiers' boots. My father came home on leave from France on some occasions and we made the best of it under the circumstances. After one of these leaves my mother and I heard nothing of my father for a very long time, and he was reported as being missing. Actually my father had fallen into a shell crater and broken his ankle. He was brought in and other things developed from it, and my father was sent from one place to another. Eventually a batch of letters arrived with the good news that my father was well.

A lot of the soldiers left the forts and work became very much less. I had a friend that worked the lime-light at the Hippodrome theatre in Portsmouth; a vacancy occurred to work one of the lime-lights in the gods, otherwise the gallery. My friend suggested that I should try for the job, but I said, 'I know nothing much about lime-lights.'

'Have a go,' he said, 'I can soon put you in the way.'

To my surprise I got the job and, with the help of my friend, soon acquired the knowledge of doing it.

By 1917 the U-boat menace, by some invention, was stopped, and the war turned in our favour on all fronts. I was fast approaching military age and I tried to join the Royal Flying Corps, but was politely told I was too old; however, with my friend from the Hippodrome I enlisted into the Royal Naval Air Service; I had to sign on for four years' active and four years on the reserve.

Chapter 4

Fort Tregantle; Blandford depot; lifted from Hell to Heaven; Nature's gentleman; I join the Blackbirds Concert Party; drafted to France; cancelled isolation; Scampton Aerodrome; dispersed leave; back to Blandford; Leuchars Aerodrome; North Queensferry; I start cooking

My friend and I were sent to Crystal Palace, London, to sign on, but he was drafted away before me. I still remained at Crystal Palace. Then I was posted to Tregantle Fort, Cornwall. Our pay was a shilling a day, but after allotment and insurance was deducted, it ran out at four shillings a fortnight. I soon knew what it was to go hungry, and some were big strapping fellows who could eat a horse. So when pay day came along the four shillings were spent in the canteen on perhaps a tin of salmon, or other things. Discipline was very severe, flogging was still in existence in the Navy, and as all were under eighteen years old, we were classed as boys. Smoking was banned; anyone caught smoking had the birch. Although I smoked I never took a chance; very rarely anyone broke this rule; there might be the odd one caught; if so the medical officer was present and the Master-at-Arms used to administer the punishment, and it took about a week for the unfortunate individual to get over it.

I don't know whether it was intuition or premonition,

call it what you like, but when I joined the services, I packed a dress suit and some conjuring apparatus in my kit; and this was to be my saviour later on. Fort Tregantle was a desolate spot, being an old fort situated on a cliff overlooking the sea. To make life a bit more cheerful I entertained the boys with conjuring. Whilst I was at Tregantle Fort, the R.F.C. and the R.N.A.S. amalgamated, forming the Royal Air Force. An option was given to join the Navy or automatically transfer into the R.A.F. As far as I know they all went for the R.A.F., including myself. Tregantle Fort closed down, and the whole lot of the personnel was sent to Blandford transit camp. I can remember it was a cold, miserable wet day, and on arrival there all the kit-bags and hammocks were piled in a heap on the downs. Particulars were taken and accommodation in various huts was found. Going back to get my kit, I could only find my hammock. I hunted for my kit-bag, containing all my cleaning gear, working clothes and other things, without result. All I had was what I stood up in.

At the time, the R.A.F. came under military administration, and the Sergeant-Major of the section I was in, although I do not like the expression, but there is no other word for it, but to describe him as a bastard. I was put on a job of white washing the posts and fences around the camp. As I had no overalls I got somewhat splashed with whitewash, and on appearing on parade in this state, immediately the Sergeant-Major pounced on me. I tried to explain that my kit had gone astray, but I might as well have spoken to a brick wall. He told me to wash, shave and wash the uniform that I had on and report to him in half-an-hour. This was almost impossible. I knew he was itching to put me on a charge.

I was sitting on my bed trying to think what could be done; time was slipping by and all I could see was jankers (service term for punishment) staring me in the face. At that moment a corporal came into the hut. 'Is your name Taylor?' he exclaimed, and for a moment I thought I was in further trouble. I told him that was my name. He said, 'I'm Nature's Gentleman', which indeed he proved to be. Somehow this rung a bell. I had seen that name billed on the music halls. 'I hear you do some conjuring. Have you any props with you?' Then I remembered I had packed my dress suit and the conjuring props in my hammock. This was a God-send, in fact a miracle.

'Oh yes! I am a professional,' I exclaimed.

'Would you like to join a concert party?'

With this I pricked up my ears. 'I would, very much so, but I am on the carpet.' I explained the situation I was in and he said, 'Never mind the Sergeant-Major. Do a trial turn in the institute. I'll see to him', and left me to get ready.

Then the thought struck me: I wonder if this is a hoax. However, I took the bull by the horns, unlashed my hammock (for I had never used it from the day of issue), took from it the conjuring gear and the dress suit, which was in a sorry state. I borrowed someone's razor, cleaned up and straightened out the dress suit as best I could, for that was all I could appear in, and with my hair plastered down with water, made my way to the Institute. When I

arrived there was nobody there; had this all been a joke?
After a while the corporal came in, followed by some
Brass Hats, who took their seats. The corporal said, 'Are
you all ready?' I had no fear of doing a trial turn, I knew
my stuff, but was this real or had I fallen asleep when I
was sitting on my bed, and acting in a dream? I pinched
myself. Yes, it was me. I went through my act and after
the corporal had a bit of conversation with the Brass
Hats, they departed. He came to me and said:

'You're in, you join the Blackbirds Concert Party;
report this to your Sergeant-Major, and then come and see
me.'

On seeing this brute of a Sergeant-Major he uttered
two words: 'Get out.' I was glad that was over, and then I
saw the corporal and arranged for my lost kit to be replaced.

I had a very happy time with the Blackbirds; although
I was the only ranker, the rest being officers, I was treated
on the same level as themselves.

The Blackbirds not only performed in Blandford camp,
but outside camps as well. During the stay with the
Blackbirds, I never saw 'Nature's Gentleman', the corporal, any more, but all good things come to an end and
eventually the Blackbirds broke up, owing to so many
being drafted away.

To my satisfaction, that bully of a Sergeant-Major was
posted and a more human type of person took his place.
It was not long before I was on draft for France, but at the
last moment a fever of some sort broke out in the hut I
was in, and this stopped my draft, and I was placed in

isolation for three weeks. After this, instead of going to France I was posted with a few more to a large house in Edinburgh, Scotland. I was only there a few days before I was sent to Scampton camp in Lincoln. Now I had to settle down to my R.A.F. trade of aerofitting; my progress was fairly rapid in this direction, and very soon I became a fully qualified aero fitter. By this time the Air Ministry was formed and the administration taken out of military hands. Scampton Aerodrome was an easy-going camp and the Sergeant-Major was a decent sort of chap. He sent for me one day and said: 'I hear you are a magician; you will understand that any entertainment you do is gratuitous.'

It so happened that a batch of Americans arrived at the camp for instruction in Aeronautics. After a while, with permission from the Sergeant-Major, I arranged to do a show for them and our chaps in the canteen. A good crowd assembled, including our Sergeant-Major; towards the end of the show one of the Americans got up and made a collection in his scout-like hat, which was part of their uniform; the collection was then passed over to me. There was nothing else I could do but take the money to the Sergeant-Major. He took charge of it and said: 'Thanks very much; this will go towards the R.A.F. funds.'

On 11 November 1918, an armistice was signed with Germany. As I had three more years to do in the R.A.F. I was sent home on a month's dispersal leave. During this period my father came home from France on demobilization. I spent a very pleasant time, then a telegram arrived telling me I was to report to Blandford camp. I was not there very long before I was posted to Leuchars Aerodrome, Fifeshire, Scotland. I was there for some time, either in the workshops or on the aerodrome; then, for no reason at all, I was posted to North Queensferry, a balloon base on the north bank of the Firth of Forth, in fact just by the side of the Forth Bridge.

When I arrived there, the Sergeant-Major said: 'What did they want to send you here for? There're no planes here. I must see what I can do about you.' And very soon I and a few more were on the move to some destination unknown. Standing outside the office, with kits packed, the men were called in one by one to receive their warrants. I was the only one left waiting to be called in; then suddenly the Sergeant-Major appeared and said: 'Can you cook spuds?' I casually remarked that 'I could cook anything', for I thought this was some sort of a send-off joke, but he continued: 'Come along with me', and I followed him to the cook house. To my surprise he wanted me to cook the men's dinner. 'Have a go and get cracking,' he said and left me to it.

Cooking to me was a matter of common sense, but there were about sixty men I had to cater for and this was something out of my line. However, I got going in my way; the Sergeant-Major called back later on, and said, 'You seem to be doing all right. Do you mean to say you haven't done this before?' I replied I had some knowledge of cooking, but not for that number of men. If I can remember rightly the menu was pretty simple, being corned beef and a couple of veg., with some sort of a sweet. I learned later on that the cook and his mate had been posted away by some error, and for a time there was no replacement. The reader will have noticed that Providence provided something unusual in my favour, which of course is unexplainable.

Chapter 5

*Chef at the Officers' Mess; I organize a concert party;
the debating society; I become a hypnotist; I leave
North Queensferry; I rejoin my squadron at Gosport; the
Punch and Judy Show; I leave the service; illness; a comic
catastrophe*

I continued in the cookhouse; no replacement arrived. I
was there for some considerable time, and now I was well
versed in the art of cooking. One day the officer of the
rounds as usual visited the cookhouse. I had for sweet
jam tart laid on the table; he tasted a bit of it, and said,
'That's better than we get.' Soon after, a cook arrived at
the camp and I was sent to the Officers' Mess, the cook
there having left.

For a small camp I found there was an abundance of
talent; it only wanted someone like myself to organize an
excellent concert party. This I did, and a very successful
concert party was formed and, with the help of an ex-
painter and decorator, the necessary scenery was painted
to requirement. Very soon an officer was placed in charge
of the party and with his authority the party went from
place to place with great success. I remember painting a
front drop cloth; it was in the form of a set of front tabs,
blue in colour, with the albatross, the R.A.F. crest,
suspended on chains in the centre; this was painted with
a sort of luminous yellow paint.

This started other camps producing concert parties, under an officer, and I think this established an entertainments officer in all camps. Apart from the concert party, I created a debating society; about a dozen chaps, including myself, would get together in an empty hut and debate upon any chosen subject.

It so happened that Dr Walford Bodie, a hypnotist, came to the Empire Theatre, Dunfermline, which was about six miles from the camp, and it was decided that a visit to the theatre to witness his display of hypnotism would provide a splendid subject for discussion. The curtain went up displaying an array of electrical apparatus; during the show Dr Bodie asked for volunteers to come up and be hypnotized. Readily, I and a few more went on the stage. I was foremost and Dr Bodie told me to sit in a chair, and suddenly I had a shock of electricity, which made me jump up in the air. I had several more shocks in various ways, and my colleagues, seeing what I was undergoing, gradually disappeared from the stage; and of course I did as well, leaving Dr Bodie with his subjects. To finish off his show Dr Bodie placed a girl in the electric chair, and she was supposed to take ten thousand volts of electricity through her body so that when Dr Bodie went near her he drew enormous sparks from her. Of course, the girl was unharmed, as static electricity only was used, but it was good entertainment.

As regards hypnotism, I was rather a sceptic; the discussion took place as arranged, and I suggested it was just a display of electrical magic; to demonstrate this, I went through a farcical form of hypnotizing one of the others.

To my astonishment he remained in a sort of stupor; I didn't know what really to do, so I said 'Wake up'; he did and solemnly declared that he had been to sleep. I tried this out with another, with the same result; this made me think there was something in hypnotism after all, so I sent away for some books on the subject, and I religiously studied hypnotism. After a time, I became very proficient at it; there was no lack of subjects in the service and, to make it much easier, they were used to commands. Under hypnotic conditions, subjects would act according to my commands. If I suggested to a subject that he was riding a horse or washing a baby, this became a reality to him, and he acted accordingly. Besides the entertainment value, cures could be effected by suggestion, such as toothache, headache or forms of nervous condition; it is now in common use by the medical profession. Stage performances have somewhat faded out, owing to some hypnotists who have been sued for damages, by causing harmful effects on certain people. Although I never became a professional in the art of hypnotism, I can honestly say that I never produced anything detrimental to my subjects; on the contrary, they came to me for the beneficial results gained from my acquired knowledge.

During my stay at North Queensferry I had letters from home informing me that my father had built a Punch and Judy Show; my parents also wanted to know when I was coming home on leave. I had now assumed the title of chef in the Officers' Mess, which by the way was a very large house, containing besides other accommodation, six bathrooms. When I approached the President of the Mess about leave, it was the same old story that I couldn't be spared, and so this went on, until the lovely little camp was closed down. I alone turned the key in the lock of the empty house, which was once the Officers' Mess, and after two years returned to Leuchars, to join my squadron, which was waiting to undergo torpedo trials at Fort Grange, Gosport, Portsmouth. There was some sort of an inquiry why I had been sent to North Queensferry, but as usual this was shelved, and I was sent to Fort Grange to join the squadron. This could not be better. I was home.

Meanwhile my parents had taken over a public house, known as the Golden Sceptre, on the Hard at Portsmouth. It was not a flourishing business at first, and my father continued in the show line. I picked up the leave that was due to me, and I had a go at learning the Punch and Judy Show. It was more difficult than I thought. I had to master the voice of Punch, which is accomplished by a small instrument known as a 'call' in the profession. It was nothing more or less than a piece of tape between two pieces of metal, usually made of silver, in case you happened to swallow it; on several occasions I nearly had this misfortune. However, after much practice I was capable of using the 'call', and also of mimicking the voices required for the figures. After about three months, the torpedo trials were finished, and I returned to Leuchars with the others.

My time in the service was nearly completed; towards the end I did some guard duties; the weather was atrocious, and I was wet through on several occasions, and I

[37]

was not feeling too grand. However, in January 1922 I was discharged from the service.

On arriving home I was really ill and collapsed. I was immediately put to bed, and the doctor called. I had double pneumonia, congestion of the lungs, pleurisy and patches of tuberculosis. In those years double pneumonia was a killer without any other complaint, and so I lingered on without the remotest chance of recovery; but one night pain and the coughing ceased and I drifted into a peaceful sleep. I awoke next morning feeling really fine. I got out of bed, walked around; I could not remember if anything had happened. The doctor called and he was really astonished; he was a blunt type of doctor, and said: 'I expected to see you in a wooden jacket this morning. How are you feeling?'

'Quite well,' I replied.

'You have been through a very critical time,' he said.

After an examination, there was still some fluid and the patches of tuberculosis to be removed. This the doctor put right and remarked, 'Your lungs are as sound as a bell, if you look after yourself and get out in the fresh air, you should not have any more serious illness.' His words have come true; I have not had any serious illness since, apart from the common cold. Providence slipped in once more and to the relief of my parents I soon regained my strength.

My first experience, after my illness, in the show line, I look back on as a comical catastrophe. An engagement for a Punch and Judy Show at a church party was accepted; apparently what was to be the main item in the programme was a sketch by some of the church members.

The Punch and Judy Show was for the younger generation. There was hardly any space at the side of the stage to build up the show, but somehow this was managed and it went down very well indeed, not only with the children, but the adults enjoyed it as well. The Punch Show was taken to the side and the sketch players in period costumes waited to go on. I could see the old vicar in the front row, rubbing his hands, his face beaming with delight; perhaps his favourite lady was taking the lead, who knows? There was great excitement at the side-wings, then the producer shouted out: 'All on.'

In the centre of the stage was a table laid out for tea; about half a dozen or more sat at this table, going through their lines. I started to pull down the Punch and Judy Show at the side, using a pair of steps, but unfortunately I touched one of the side-wings, which had a thick coat of dust on it. This must have just been on the balance; I tried to grab it, as it went over, but it was just beyond my reach. I shouted, but too late. Plonk! it went in a cloud of dust, right on those at the table. There were screams, arms and legs protruded from under the wing; the vicar rushed on the stage followed by others, out came smelling salts; it looked comical with wigs knocked at an angle on their heads, but not so funny at the time. When order was restored, my father and I packed up the show and apologized to the vicar; but he just fixed my father and me with a stony stare, so a quick exit was made. I did not have the nerve to send in for the fee (for I did the business side of the work), so a show was, to speak in show business terms, done for the king.

Chapter 6

My father and I travel on cycles; experience with a gang of crooks; the queer inn; the show at Egham; the Pandeau pipes; an accident; I buy a car; Punch and Judy Shows at schools; Christmas in London; 'In the Jungle'; an audition for the music-halls; 'Strangers'; Phil Vine

It was decided to leave the show line for a time, and devote more time to the pub; but my father was a showman, and a showman he remained. I was a showman and not too keen about the public-house line; however, I took part in the business and mostly did the cellar work. Although my mother was a business woman to her finger tips, it took a long time to work the business up, other sources of income had to be found, and the show business proved the only means.

I booked two or three fêtes, one at Dorking and the other two at a place called Egham in Surrey. The means of transport was to fix a trailer to a cycle I had, with a box-like arrangement, to carry the Punch and Judy Show and other props. Attached to the back of my father's cycle was a tow rope, which could be hooked on the box of the trailer, to help me up hills. This wild idea was carried out, and my father and I set out on the journey to Dorking. It was a hard journey, but we made it, I thoroughly tired out. A few days were spent at Dorking with relatives before resuming the journey to Egham.

At the time I wished that I had never thought of this idea of conveyance, and that we had used public transport instead; but the venture was on, and it had to be carried through. Arriving at Egham, a very quiet, select place on the Thames, it seemed just one main road, with hardly anyone walking in it, and most likely about one policeman looked around, if he wasn't having a nap. The thing was to get put up for a week somewhere.

In the centre of the main drag stood an old coaching inn, by the name of the George Inn. What I am going to relate now sounds more like a thriller than an auto-biography, but the old axiom 'Truth is stranger than fiction' in this case is appropriate. My father and I entered this inn and ordered a couple of drinks. The land-lady, a hard-faced, thin-lipped woman about sixty, with dark suspicious-looking eyes, served the drinks. On inquiry about accommodation, she must have taken my father and me for a couple of roadsters. I quickly explained the situation to her, and she reluctantly replied, 'You can have a bed, no breakfast, and I want the money', and held her hand out to receive it. She would not have it any other way but nightly. Under the circumstances this was gladly accepted, as far as I was concerned. I was dead tired and slept like a log.

Next morning, I noticed the floor of the room through the years had sunk at one end and the only place for the bed was at that end, but what fascinated me most was a large hook in the ceiling directly over the bed; whether this was a store, I don't know, but everything seemed queer about the room; nevertheless, after having some breakfast at some restaurant, we arrived at the fête with the gear and fixed the Punch and Judy up; besides this my father did some magic. There was quite a good number of people there and the show went down well. Arriving back at the inn, the landlady held out her hand and uttered one word: 'Money.'

Next night I did not sleep so well, for there was the sound of high-powered cars running in and out the yard. I mentioned this to my father and he said he had heard them as well; but what gave me a big surprise was when I had reason late one night to go to the toilet, which was situated in the yard, and I was startled by a grunt. I was nearly struck dumb, for there was an iron cage with the largest gorilla or ape in it I ever saw. I went back and found my father awake; on telling him what I had seen, he said, 'You're dreaming; go to sleep.'

Next morning I insisted on what I saw, but my father said, 'When I see it, I'll believe it'; so it went on: cars in and out during the night, and the landlady holding out her hand and saying the one word, 'Money'.

I still gazed at the hook over the bed, wondering what it could have been used for, so I plucked up courage one night, and asked the landlady about the hook. She replied, 'A man hung himself from it once.' This was very comforting; I wondered if she did or didn't want my father and me there.

To find other accommodation was not possible, because the show took up most of the time. Eventually this landlady seemed to soften a bit, even so far as to offer food. Her attitude changed to one of friendliness, but she made a strange remark, saying, 'What you see and hear here, I advise you to keep a still tongue in your heads; the gentlemen would like you to entertain them this evening.'

It was then that I suspected that a gang operated from this place. Why was it then that she had accommodated my father and me? Was it for the money or because entertainers could be useful to them? I asked myself the question, but could not supply the answer; however, I thought it wise to do what they requested. The landlady took my father and me across the yard to a large room; inside were two billiard tables, and assembled there was a number of immaculately dressed men. No introduction was needed, they knew all about my father and me; evidently every move had been watched, or the landlady had supplied the information. The show was greatly appreciated; with many taps on the back and what are you going to have in the way of drinks. One of them said, 'You have seen our little pet, the ape; very useful fellow for keeping away intruders at night.' I was now convinced they were a gang of crooks.

The shows were over at Egham and, before leaving, the landlady presented my father and me with a fairly large sum of money saying, 'For your services; the gentlemen liked you very much; hoping to see you again.' The money was accepted, for, after all, the show work wasn't done for fun. On leaving, the landlady repeated the warning about keeping quiet about things. Only too glad to get away, my father and I proceeded back to Dorking.

Arriving back at Dorking, the rest of the day was spent

[43]

resting. The last fête was at Bookham, about six or seven miles from Dorking. The secretary was a very nice gentleman; arrangements were made to have the Punch Show a little way from the main attractions, in order that a crowd of children would not interfere so much with other things. To draw the children to the show my father would play the drum and Pandeau pipes, at which he was a master.

A word about the Pandeau pipes for those who have not heard or seen them. It was an instrument made from canes, cut to various lengths, the longest being about nine inches, and the shortest about two inches, the centres being removed; the pipes were then placed in a pan of warm fat and soaked, to make them mellow; the canes were then taken out, and bound together by two crosspieces in order of length. In order to produce the various notes small plugs of cork were pushed inside the canes up or down. To tune these, the middle C of a piano was struck until the pitch of the longest pipe corresponded, the other notes followed suit in accordance with two octaves towards the treble part of the keyboard. To play this instrument it was necessary to puff down the pipes, and at the same time draw it along the lips; it took considerable practice to produce a tune, but when this was accomplished the shrill tones could be heard for some distance.

This fête was a very posh affair: there were Russian dancers, an operatic society and big singers of the day; a large marquee with a stage decked with floral arrangements was also provided. I believe the secretary's name

[44]

was Mr Eyles; anyway he was also an entertainer; his act was to draw cartoons on sheets of paper and to spin a funny story about them. It was very clever. Besides the Punch and Judy Show and the act of Mr Eyles, my father was to present a ventriloquial act with the figure, which by the way he had added to his achievements, and I was to do a magic show, so this constituted the variety show or party.

My father and I put on the dress suits as usual and the show opened up. His Majesty King George V and Queen Mary paid a visit to the fête. If only the Punch and Judy Show had been situated nearer, and I could have put up the figures for them, I could have had the royal coat of arms over the show, but after seeing the main attractions His Majesty and the Queen departed. The operatic Russian dancers and singers were the stars of the show, or were they? I didn't much care for them, for they were extremely snobbish. I liked Eyles very much; he was friendly and like my father and me. The variety show proved more popular than the other party and they did not like this very much.

On the last day of the show something went wrong with the free wheel of my father's cycle, so he had to stay the night at Bookham. I decided to ride back to Dorking, and pick up the props the following day. I found the trailer more difficult to ride when it was unloaded, and as I was entering Dorking, riding fairly fast, I lost control of the cycle and ran into a low brick wall. I shot over the top and landed right in a large pile of animal manure. There was no damage hardly, except that the trailer was bent slightly; but did I smell – that wasn't the word for it! My aunt immediately prepared a bath for me and I had a change of clothes.

The next day, back at Bookham, I told my father of my accident, and he laughed like blazes. The trailer was loaded up, and my father and I started on the journey to Portsmouth. It was a terrible day, raining, fog and the journey seemed never-ending. Arriving at Portsmouth my father and I were exhausted, and the cycles were put away. We had had enough of cycling, and they were never used again. Soon after, I bought a second-hand T Ford, and after getting a licence at the Post Office for five shillings (for there was no test or compulsory insurance then), I had to learn to drive it in one try-out. I had a run with the fellow whom I bought it from, and he said, 'Well, that's how it's done', and left me to it. I got the hang of it after some practice in a side road; the object was to work the schools round about, and this was to be the means of conveyance, which was certainly better than cycling.

Some small bills were printed with the words, 'Bring one penny with this bill for a Punch and Judy and magic entertainment'. The headmaster had full power, in those days, to arrange anything he wanted at a school; mostly he gave sanction for the show to take place the same day or another date. On the day of the entertainment my father and I would stand by the gate of the playground at about twelve o'clock and, as the children came out, we distributed the bills. Generally the show would be arranged to start at 3 P.M. in the schoolroom, and nearly all the children would be present. The headmaster would then address them with words to this effect: 'Mr Taylor has arranged to give you a Punch and Judy Show and conjuring performance. I want you to be especially alert to the conjuring he is going to show you, for I am going to get you to write an essay on the show and try to give your reasons as to how the tricks are done.' With this he would watch the performance through, probably enjoying it as much as the children. After the show the headmaster would say something like, 'That will give them something to think about.' The schools were always a good stand-by, especially when there was nothing else on.

Magic, like most arts, requires much practice, either with a professional or in front of a mirror, as an audience would see you. When you first start to acquire the art of magic, you have to decide what style you are going to adopt. My aim is a conversational style, in which I talk to the audience, using jokes, gags and comedy. Another style is where the performer deliberately makes a mess of his tricks, such as the act Tommy Cooper puts over; and then there is the silent or dumb performer, who does not speak, but adopts a graceful style of movement. Accompanied by soft music, he enters, removing his top hat, cloak and gloves and usually throws his cane to the side, where it is caught by a stage hand, or suddenly changes the cane into a couple of handkerchiefs. He then proceeds to manipulate the cards, billiard balls and cigarettes and ends by producing something startling, such as a very large pipe. An assistant then comes on, gives the magician his top hat and replaces his cloak; the performer puts on his gloves and gracefully takes the curtain. This kind of act is very popular since it can be performed in any country, without language problems.

Every year my father and I did six weeks' performance at a London store, just before Christmas. The performance, which was about twenty minutes in duration, ended by producing Father Christmas with his sack of toys from an empty cabinet. It was intended for my father to take the part of Father Christmas; he had the right build for such a part, and the cabinet was constructed to his size. I remember on the first opening at this store some misunderstanding was made concerning Father Christmas; they had their own chap selected for the job. He was the caretaker and over six feet tall, and seemingly impossible to produce from the cabinet; but he insisted on having a try. The cabinet was constructed with a secret panel at the back, and that was all there was to it; the person would stand behind the panel whilst the front was shown empty, then a curtain was drawn and the person would come through the panel; the whole cabinet was turned round and, when the curtain was withdrawn, the person would appear. How this caretaker reduced his size, I don't know, but he did it, and when produced towered nearly head and shoulders over the cabinet; this, indeed, made it more effective.

It was a happy trio, my father, George (the caretaker), and myself; we had a special room to dine together, for all the catering was done on the premises.

The shows finished up at Christmas Eve, and it was

arranged that George, my father, and I should celebrate at the local that night, which unwisely took place. As the premises were all locked up at night, it was also arranged that on Christmas Day my father and I should climb the fire escape, which was in three or four sections, to the old cook's kitchen, where she would have the window open for us to enter, and she would have something special laid on.

Christmas morning my father and I had terrible hangovers from the night before, and to make it worse, it was raining, as one would say, cats and dogs; however, we managed to climb the fire-escape, and entered through the open window where George and the old cook were waiting to pass on the usual greetings. She certainly did have something laid on, not only did she load us up with sandwiches, but in the tea was a liberal dose of whisky, and plenty more if it was wanted. After this my father and I were considerably revived, and bidding farewell to them had no idea that this would be the last time there, for the firm went into liquidation.

I had to drive home to Portsmouth that morning; it was not until Petersfield was reached that the weather broke into sunshine. After Christmas, the usual New Year festivities took place, and for many years the Royal Naval Barracks engaged my father and me for entertainment.

We were also engaged by Storry's, the pianoforte firm of Portsmouth. On one occasion the manager of this firm said, 'There is a call for home cinema shows, I know where there is one for sale if you are interested.' He gave the address and the projector and equipment were purchased. With it there was a resistance. I wired this up to the best of my knowledge, and it seemed to work all right at home. Among the films was a fairly dark one called *In the Jungle*. An engagement for a cinema show from Storry's was accepted. The place was just outside Chichester, and as it was visited in the past by royalty it was well known. Unfortunately the van was in dock with some trouble, so it was arranged that my father and I were to be met at Chichester station by their car and conveyed to the place.

On arrival, I commenced to rig up the projector and it goes to prove that a little knowledge of electrical business is dangerous. I was unaware at the time that the place was on direct current. I wired up the resistance, as I thought, and switched it on: there was a flash, and the place was plunged into darkness. The chauffeur happened to be on the spot, and it was a good job he was, for he fixed the fuses, and once more there was light, but I had no light for the cinema projector; however the chauffeur, a decent fellow, said he had a battery to spare, which with his aid was wired up to the projector, although it was really not powerful enough.

The children and adults took their places around the screen and I started the show, but to my horror I found that I had fixed the dark film, *In the Jungle*, and as it was dark, hardly a thing could be discerned on the screen. There were remarks like, 'What's it all about, Mama', 'I can't see a thing'. All I could say was, 'It's in the jungle; it will be lighter in a minute.' The other films were not much better, and when the show was over they silently sauntered out. I wished that I had never set eyes on the projector.

My father and I packed up as quick as possible and got away. The next day my father and I were called to Storry's. The manager was furious. He said, 'What happened? She won't pay.' This didn't surprise me in the least. I told him that I had had trouble with the projector, and could not put it right there and then, and did the best thing I could. I admitted the show was a flop. The manager exclaimed: 'She is a good customer. I don't want to lose her. Can you put it right?' 'Certainly,' I said; whether I could or not remained to be seen.

He there and then rang her up, explaining that the projector had gone wrong at the critical moment, and apologized concerning the show; but if she would like to arrange another date, it would be replaced by another projector, and the firm would stand all expenses. She was very reluctant about this, but eventually consented to arrange a date later on. I wasn't very keen to go back there; if it had been Punch and Judy, ventriloquism or magic, it would have been a success. However, I did away with the resistance, and wired it direct to a twelve-volt accumulator, and it threw a splendid picture. She arranged another date, Storry's assured her that everything was all right. The van was out of dock, I returned there with a better heart, and the show was a great success. I did a number of shows for the firm and nothing went wrong again.

Now, my father and I thought it time to have a go at the music-halls, so a double comedy act, using the cabinet that produced Father Christmas, came into play. It was well rehearsed and perfect in every detail. An audition was arranged with a so-called London agent, and if ever my father and I were caught on the hop, it was then. The audition was held in nothing more or less than a large pub in Bayswater. It had a bit of a stage with curtain one end and a small room off for a dressing-room. There were several artistes there awaiting an audition. The agent was there and in business-like manner interviewing the various turns. A more hostile type of audience couldn't be imagined. Some turns went on before my father and me; they were booed, jeered at and perhaps an occasional clap, it was nothing more than a mob taking the micky out of the artistes. One poor chap went on (I admit he was pretty weak) and started to sing, 'It ain't going to rain no more, no more', and I remember it was pouring down in torrents outside. He was jeered, booed at and pelted with missiles; he never finished his song. I refused to go on, but the agent said, 'It's quite all right, I'll call order'; this eventually he did. My father and I went through the act. Apart from one or two boos, we had a fairly good round of applause, which was more than some of the other artistes had.

After the show, the agent came to us and said, 'I know the audience is a pretty tough one, but if you go well here, you will do well anywhere. I'll fix up a contract for you two boys. Call on me in a day or so', and handed us his card with his agency address, somewhere in Charing Cross. I smelt a rat concerning the business; it proved to be right, for the address was a fictitious one, and no agent or office ever existed. The idea was to advertise for would-be artistes, to have an audition, providing a cheap evening's entertainment, and the bogus agent must have had a rake-off from the landlord. With all our experience of show work, how my father and I fell for this one, I don't know.

After visiting some more agents the act was booked up for a road show, run by a very well-known comedienne. It was a good show, but the title of the show, *Strangers*, seemed a very dull one, and hardly a box office draw name. However, my father and I went on tour with them, but it was up and down; sometimes she could only pay half salary with a promise. The show came to the Grand Theatre, Brighton. There was terrific opposition there: George Robey on at the Hippodrome and several cinemas showing *The Gold Diggers of Broadway*. *Strangers* was playing to empty houses. At the end of the week, she called the artistes to her dressing-room, and I felt very sorry for her for she was in tears, and said, 'I can only pay you half salary. Owing to financial difficulties the show is finished.'

My father and I returned to Portsmouth, and had to settle in the pub for a time, owing to the difficult times the country was experiencing: unemployment and general unrest, things were indeed bad. Eventually this culminated in the General Strike of 1926. After the strike, and with things more settled, a great friend of my father's, whose name was Phil Vine, came round and suggested a brilliant idea of making some quick money. The show line was quiet for a time. His idea was to have the van painted in a bright colour, with the words *free sample* in large lettering on both sides of the van. Then uniforms of a type were procured, and some small hand bills printed with the words, 'Get your free sample of Weights Gold Medal Herb Beans, at the van. Bring one penny with this bill for the cost of packing'. About a dozen of these beans were placed in small wage packets and sealed, so it was not a swindle; it was the wording on the bills that did the trick. These beans were particularly good; they must have contained cayenne pepper; one bean alone would set you on fire.

Although this was out of my line, I thought I would give it a try. Donning the uniforms and driving the van into a side road or street, just off a main road, two of us would stand by the van giving out the bills to passing people, whilst the other one would remain in the van, with the back doors opened containing some sort of a counter. As soon as people read the bills the psychological effect was amazing. Out came the pennies, and those who did not read the bill followed suit for the free sample. In no time the floor of the van was covered in pennies; there was no time to give change, the money came in too fast and was thrown down without hesitation.

This, indeed, was a quick way of making money, so we went on moving from one street to another. I remember taking the van to Poole; my father had other business on, so he did not come. It started to rain very hard and the van was at a street corner when a policeman came along. 'Here, what's all this?' he exclaimed. Phil Vine explained that it was an advertising stunt giving away free samples,

Myself, aged fifteen; my father and mother

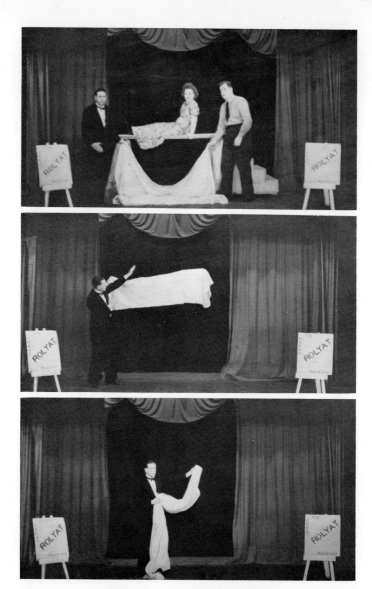

Three views of a vanishing lady

and offered him a packet of the beans. Instead of taking one, the policeman emptied the contents of the packet into his mouth. I have already remarked how hot they were. He coughed, spluttered and nearly choked, the expression on his face was comical. After he rallied round, he exclaimed, 'I have a good mind to put you in charge for giving away dangerous sweets', which, of course, he said more or less in a joke. As he went away he said, 'They ain't half bloody hot.'

For some reason or the other, for a time, the manufacture of the herbal beans ceased. I decided to manufacture my own cough tablets, so I looked through a book of remedies and discovered a formula to make a very good tablet, the basis of which was liquorice powder. After studying the process I produced a very good lozenge. These went very well.

My father and I came in contact with a young Jew, a sort of playboy, good natured, with plenty of money to burn. He liked to come with my father and me just for the excitement. He was known as Teddy, so the company increased to four. At Basingstoke I pulled the van up outside the picture palace; at the time my father was in the van and Teddy, Phil Vine and I were outside with the bills. Coming towards the picture palace was a procession of people, of various ages in a blue type of uniform. When they got nearer one could see they were mental cases; though it was not right of Teddy and Phil Vine, they thought to play a joke on my father by giving these people some bills, and telling them to go to the van where they would be given a gold watch. This disorganized the procession; they got round the van, mixed up with other people, demanding gold watches. My father shouted out that there were no gold watches given away. Eventually my father closed the doors of the van, and the person in charge started to round them up, and got them on their way. Another time Teddy brought some hard-boiled eggs and continually cracked them on Phil Vine's bald pate. Phil kept on saying, 'Don't do that, Teddy.' These two were always up to some joke or the other, but still it kept things cheerful. So this went on until other vans doing the same thing appeared on the scene, and so it was decided to finish with it; the money was had whilst the going was good.

Chapter 7

Around the halls with the cinematograph; the explosion; the pillory illusion; booking a band; the band gets inebriated up the Rhondda Valley; Ben, the blink fencer; back to Oxford; back to Portsmouth

The pub was doing much better, but there was more money in the show business, so my father and I remained in it. It was decided to run a cinematograph show, with magic, Punch and Judy, ventriloquism, and a fellow named Curly, a brilliant pianist; so the projector was produced, another one purchased and a full-size screen was made from two sheets with a black border around the edge. The intention was to hire village halls for one or two nights in accordance. As some halls still used oil lamps, a large acetylene plant was bought, fixed by a flexible tube to a metal tube containing burners for footlights. The plant was stood outside a side window, owing to the smell. Another smaller acetylene generator was manufactured by my father out of a seven-pound sweet tin. The screen was on rollers, so as to act as a front drop. Bills were printed, to be displayed in shops, and on any hoardings; a complimentary ticket to the show was issued to those displaying the bills. Curly, the pianist, acted as advance agent. Halls were booked, and the show went on the road. For the sake of the children, an earlier show was arranged of Punch and Judy.

As shows of this description seldom visited the villages, it was an instant success. Curly was the biggest scrounger I knew, mostly to the advantage of all; he would disappear for a time, returning with a large jug of tea, and tray full of bread and butter and cakes. At first I said, 'How much did that cost?' 'Nothing,' he replied, 'just a complimentary ticket.'

One of the halls booked was at Hedge End, near Southampton, and getting ready for the evening show my father was in front of the hall whilst I was in a dressing-room. All of a sudden there was a terrific bang, and white dust was blown everywhere. I rushed out and saw my father smothered in white dust as though a sack of flour had been emptied over him. Although standing in an upright position he was stunned and out. When he came to, and I found he was not hurt, I asked him what had happened. Apparently he had been adjusting the small acetylene generator. He said, 'I lit a match to have a smoke, and that is all I remember.' The seven-pound sweet tin had been blown flat, as if a steam roller had been over it. How he escaped injury is beyond me. The caretaker rushed over, thinking that one of his high-pressure lamps had exploded. The place was smothered in carbide dust. What a mess to clean up! Curly was away at the time getting the tea boat and, I can tell you, tea never tasted better.

After this refreshment it took a considerable time to clean up the mess. This was done, and the evening show took place as usual.

At home, among the props, I dug out a stand-up pillory illusion. This consisted of a flat base, with two battens, supporting two boards hinged at one side. The boards had three round holes cut in them, one for the head of a person, and the other two for the hands. On the other end was a large padlock and hasp. When the boards were opened the person would place his head and hands in the half holes, the top board was then closed over the person and padlocked; the person was a complete prisoner, or so it seemed. The whole apparatus had been painted a brilliant red. The Pillory was enclosed by a cabinet with a front curtain. Inside the cabinet were bells, tambourines, drum, whistle and anything to kick up a row.

The idea was to present a spiritualistic demonstration. I would be locked in the Pillory, the curtain drawn and tambourines would fly over the top of the cabinet, drums beat, a real right pandemonium would take place and, when the curtain was drawn, I was still locked in the Pillory. A person would be invited from the audience to go into the cabinet with me; of course, I was still locked up, and after a brief time he came rushing out, with braces hanging down, his shirt out, coat turned inside out, and off he went.

This created roars of laughter, but so simple was the mystery, in fact there was no secret at all, it was superb showmanship. I have small hands and, by screwing them up, I could draw them through the holes; so absurd, no one thought this possible; having withdrawn my hands I was free to obtain a duplicate key, unlock the padlock and perform the various antics with the articles in the cabinet.

In presenting the Pillory, my father would go amongst the audience and notice a person with rather large hands, and invite that person to be locked in the Pillory to prove the impossibility of getting out. Naturally enough he couldn't, his hands were too large. The member of the audience to enter the cabinet was none other than Curly with a false moustache; he mingled with the audience, and was foremost in coming on the stage, and acted his part accordingly.

The show was directed towards Oxford, and contact was made with friends of my father, who were musicians, so a band of about five travelled with the show. Athough there was no female turn, the cinematograph made up for any shortcomings. Sometimes the band went out and played at various spots to advertise the show. On one occasion they went out, but mostly advertised the show around the pubs, and when the evening performance came round they were, as you would say, 'well oiled'. The conductor made his entry by staggering on to the stage and falling over the music-stand; the band played in a very erratic manner and this was taken by the audience as part of the act, and produced roars of laughter. My father was very annoyed about this, and threatened to do without their services; however it was patched up, and it never happened again; but although the drunk act was rehearsed for the laughter it created, it was never so realistic. Summer-time came along; this being a bad time for booking halls, the show packed up and the company went their various ways. Back at Portsmouth a stand was arranged on Southsea beach. My father and I brushed up on the second-sight, whilst he did the conjuring. The weather as far back as I can remember was variable. Five or six shows were put on in a day, and the season passed uneventfully.

After the summer months, a short run of halls were booked up the Rhondda Valley, South Wales. This was for two turns of second sight and magic during the programme of flicks (moving pictures so called in those days). The journey by the van was taken via Oxford, where a stay with relatives was had for a few days. At Oxford I had an Uncle Jack Allen, a general dealer, who had a large amount of ground on which he also kept pigs. My uncle was a rough-cut diamond with a heart of gold. He always had a pot of soup on the hob, from which, with his fingers, he pulled bits of meat and fat asunder. How he used to get it down, I don't know; it properly turned my stomach.

The journey to South Wales was resumed and arriving there we got fixed up with digs and opened out at the first picture palace. The landlady was an old theatrical pro. Her husband played in a street band. She was a big brawny woman, and every week-end she went busking around the pubs, singing and playing a guitar, and I might say, they were a tough lot, the miners. She came back one night with her guitar busted up; apparently a miner tried to take a liberty with her, and she promptly hit him over the head with her guitar. My father repaired it for her. The husband was a sarcastic little man, and she said to him, 'That's more than you can do, you worm.'

The miner in those days was paid on a contract, that is so many tons of coal shifted at a price agreed on. When this amount was removed the miner would get a lump sum of sixty, eighty or even a hundred pounds in accordance. Those on night shift, when they came up and got their money, went straight to the boozer for a drink up, and a sing-song, for which the Welsh are noted. It happened to be one of these times; my father and I were in a pub, when one came in and my father and I knew him straight away as 'Ben, the blink fencer'. His business was selling eye-glasses, which cost him, by buying by the gross, fivepence a pair, which he sold again at an exorbitant price. A crowd of miners came in and Ben got to business. First of all he produced his chart of letters – some small, some larger. He picked on one of the miners, and asked him if he could read the smallest letters, but held it at such a distance away that anyone with fairly good eyesight would have difficulty in reading them. After a bit of by-play Ben would say, 'I see you need glasses', whether the person did or not. He disposed of some pairs, probably for half a guinea. As one miner handled his pair the pebble fell out, and he immediately shouted, 'Fraud! Swindle!' My father and I, seeing trouble, quickly got out. The last I saw of 'Ben, the blink fencer', he was being chased by a crowd of miners.

The run of picture palaces was completed, and a return to Oxford was started. On our way a stop at Lydney in 'the Forest of Dean' was made. A fair was in progress, and a pub my father and I entered was full of tin-miners. After a drink my father could not resist the temptation of showing them a few tricks; a collection was made and we left Lydney with our pockets bulging with money.

I drove the van as far as Northleach, Gloucestershire, where a stop was made, but there was still about forty or fifty miles to go. My father and I were in a pub as usual when a party came in and, to my surprise, they were Oxford people whom I knew. 'Hullo,' they said. 'What are you doing here?' 'The same question applies to you!' I said. They had a char-a-banc outing.

The evening turned to rain and the driver said, 'You keep my tail light in view and you'll be all right.' The rain became very heavy, and I had to drive over the Wolds, a ridge of hills. Soon the tail-light of the char-a-banc became fainter and disappeared entirely. As I drove on the rain became a blinding sheet, and the visibility reduced to nothing. I stopped for a while; then, as there was no signs of it easing off, I drove on again. There was no automatic wiper, only a bar arrangement which my father continually drew across the windscreen. His arm kept blotting out my vision, and at last I said, 'There's nothing for it but to open the windscreen.' In no time my father and I were wet through, but still I drove on, trying to keep the van in the centre of the narrow road, as there was a drop on both sides.

At last I descended into Witney, on to the main road to Oxford, which was about ten miles, and wasn't I thankful? The rain had stopped by now, and I pulled in on my Uncle Jack's ground, which was at Cowley. I knocked at the door and knocked again. Then the window opened, and he shouted out, 'Who's there?' I replied, 'Vic and Ted. I've come from South Wales.' 'Come from where?' he said. 'South Wales and wet through,' I replied. 'Well, come on in, and get those clothes off and have some bloody hot soup.' And in no time a roaring fire was made up and, believe me, that soup was thoroughly enjoyed. It was in the early hours of the morning when my aunt made up a bed for my father and me and, thoroughly tired out, we fell into a beautiful sound sleep. After a good breakfast the news came through that the char-a-banc had finished up in a ditch, but no one was hurt. After a stay of a few days with relatives, a return was made to Portsmouth.

Chapter 8

*Charlotte Street of former years; I get a drenching; court-
ship and marriage*

The usual Christmas shows came along and then there
was a lapse for a time in the show line.

At this juncture it would be interesting to describe the
well-known market-place of Portsmouth, namely Charlotte Street – to the younger generation a revelation of
history, to the older people a recollection of memories. It
was a narrow street, running from Commercial Road to
Edinburgh Road, but today development has altered it
so much as to make it unrecognizable. To walk through
Charlotte Street of years ago was an education in itself;
it was crowded with people shoulder-to-shoulder milling
around the various stalls, lit up by kerosene flares which
were replaced by electric light only later on.

Towards midnight, fish and meat would be auctioned
off at give-away prices, which most of the poorer class of
people waited for. Pitches were let out to quack doctors,
corn removers, sword swallowers, rope tyers and such like
at a shilling.

One well-known quack doctor in frock coat and top hat

hired a dray and a band of four or five musicians. He purchased about a pound of soap, rolled it into pills, dusted them over with french chalk and put them in small round boxes, known as chip boxes, which he sold to cure any amount of complaints. If it did not do any good, it did not do any harm, but certainly made those who bought them move in the right direction.

This quack doctor extracted teeth, of course, without an anaesthetic. He would call for someone with a bad tooth and the person going up went behind a curtain arrangement. The band would then strike up with a loud roll on the drums to smother the yells of pain of the patient, who staggered off the platform and disappeared. The quack doctor would come forward proudly displaying the molar in his forceps. Another fellow selling cough tablets had a good gimmick. He would speak in a husky voice, coughing frequently. Someone in the crowd would shout out, 'Why don't you take one yourself, guvnor?' He would reply, 'A very good idea.' Having taken the tablet, he would exclaim in a clear loud voice: 'You see what it has done for me, it will do the same for you.' Then there was a coloured man immaculately dressed and who spoke most eloquent English. He sold tooth powder, which was nothing more or less than scented pumice powder, packed in the usual chip boxes. He would ask someone in the crowd to come forward with almost black teeth, presumably an old pipe smoker. He showed his set of gleaming teeth, exclaiming, 'With my preparation I can make this man's black teeth as white as my own in a few seconds.' Whereon he produced his handkerchief, wrapped it round his finger and dipped it into a glass of water, then in the powder, and started to rub the man's teeth. The result was startling: from black to almost pure white; but the pumice powder took off all the enamel, as one can imagine, and the man's teeth would in no time resume the same colour, if not blacker than ever.

I remember a fairly elderly man, with a broad country accent; he made a preparation of lard and pulverized soda for removing corns. This may soften them; I can't imagine it would remove them. However, he finished up by saying, 'With my preparation I have removed many corns', and diving his hand in his pockets he produced a handful of objects made from candle grease to represent the corns he had removed.

Then there was a little woman who released herself from a strait-jacket; with her was a little man, and he would make a most eloquent speech about the clever manner in which the woman escaped, but she would spoil his flowery speech by saying in a very common manner, 'Yes, I can get out of a sausage skin.' This was a very amusing event. Generally a sailor strapped her in the strait-jacket; in doing so, much of her underwear was exposed which, by the way, was a brilliant red; this caused much laughter. She rolled on the ground in all directions, and pulled all sorts of facial expressions of pain in the operation of getting out. There were shouts from the crowd such as, 'Go it, missus', and after a fake struggle she eventually emerged from the strait-jacket and a collection was made.

[67]

The fire-eaters took a mouthful of paraffin, which they blew on to lighted torches, producing a great volume of flame, a most unpleasant way of making a living. Another fellow used to swallow stones, eat glass, swallow watches and suchlike, and finishing by swallowing swords. This was quite genuine; the object was to overcome the vomiting sensation, which was achieved by placing a round stick in the mouth, and by degrees taking it down the throat, until this sensation was removed. Having accomplished this by throwing the head well back, the well-blunted sword had a straight passage to the stomach.

I mustn't leave out the man who sold hair restorer. I am unaware of what concoction he had for this; he grew his hair much farther down than his shoulders, which was a most unusual sight in those days. He produced a lemon and poured some of his preparation over it, placed it under a handkerchief and when he removed the handkerchief it was smothered in hair; obviously a bit of conjuring was employed for this.

There were old junk stalls of all descriptions, some of old broken-down furniture, second-hand clothing, old books, second-hand cycles and anything saleable.

At the end of a market day, Charlotte Street was absolutely smothered in the refuse of fruit and paper wrappers, but it was surprising how quickly this litter was cleared.

Returning to the activities of show business, my father and I decided to work over the Isle of Wight with the Punch and Judy Show during the coming summer. So the show was renovated and painted up, and a start was made. All the usual buskers were there, with banjoes, guitars, accordions and various instruments. My father and I performed at various places in the Isle of Wight, and did very well. At Ryde the tide comes right up to the promenade wall, leaving only small patches of sandy beach. It was on one of these patches that a pitch was made, but the show was still too near the water's edge. I was in the show performing when a large liner came along causing a swell so that waves pounded on the shore and, before I was aware of it, over went the show. The figures were scattered all over the place and I was drenched. I took care that this never happened again.

At times my father and I performed at Hayling Island, near Portsmouth, which had a very fine stretch of sands. During the visits there my father and I called at a small pub; the landlord was an old mechanic and often tuned the old van for us. The daughter was a kindly person and very fond of animals. She saw to it that 'Toby', the dog that took part in the show, had all it wanted. Eventually I courted this young lady and wedded her on Boxing Day, 1931.

Chapter 9

Show work on Selsey Bill; pipes for a lady; a few tricks;
Find the Lady; the banknote trick; the motor accident;
trip to Oxford; slight encounter with a policeman; my
father dies

A visit to Selsey Bill on the Sussex coast was made with
the Punch and Judy Show. It was during the lunch hour
and anyone would think it was a crazy idea; there wasn't
a soul there, except for a few cars parked on some rough
ground adjoining the beach. A chap in some sort of a
uniform appeared, and my father approached him and
said, 'Do any people get here?' He replied, 'After the
lunch hour, quite a number.' Then my father went on to
say, 'Would you think it worth while to perform a Punch
and Judy Show here?' He replied, 'You have come to the
right chap. I will see what my guvnor thinks about it;
he owns the foreshore here. I will let you know in an
hour's time.' The old van was parked at the rear of the
Marina Hotel, which was situated right on the sea front,
and my father and I went into the public bar and were
surprised to find a crowd of top-line theatrical artistes
assembled there.

My father had dog Toby in his arms when one of them
came to him and said, 'That's a pretty-looking dog;
what's its name?'

'Toby,' my father replied, and he explained to this artiste what the business was.

'Fine, we get the kids down there, I'd like to see the old show.'

'But,' said my father, 'permission hasn't been granted yet.'

After having a drink with them, my father and I went back to the beach and, sure enough, the fellow in uniform was there. He said, 'The old man has given you permission to perform, providing you use his car park.' It was only a shilling on this rough ground, which was gladly accepted. It appears that the old chap he referred to was a descendant of some old Scottish king; he had a queer old house right on the front, with a crest-of-arms on the front gate and this fellow not only acted as car-park attendant, but did other business for him. After lunch a number of people assembled on the beach including all the professionals and their children.

I generally did the show and my father did the collecting; the performance went down great, everyone placed money in the bag, and it was mostly silver. One of the professionals came up and said: 'Gosh, I did enjoy the old show, especially the boxing match.'

After this my father and I appeared in dress suits and did exceedingly well. It was a gem of a place. One day the car-park attendant came up, and said, 'The old man has seen your show, and likes it very much, but he won't have any buskers here.'

My father and I became great favourites of the professionals, and whenever my father and I entered the

Marine Hotel it was: 'Hello, Punch, what are you going to have.' This was even better than the Isle of Wight, as no opposition was encountered, but a visit to Selsey Bill was only made once or twice a week, as it was residential holiday-makers that usually went there.

During a performance I happened to look round and I was startled to see the grinning head of an Indian poked through the back of the show. I finished the show and said to my father, 'What was that Indian up to, with his head stuck through the back.'

My father was all smiles and replied, 'That, my boy, was an Indian prince, and he paid well to have a look and see how it was done.'

'Oh!' I said, 'that's different.'

At Hayling Island one day a well-known titled lady approached my father and said, 'You play the Pandeau pipes exceedingly well. It is the only instrument I haven't tried. Do you know where I can get a set?'

My father replied, 'All Punch and Judy men make their own', and added that, if she would like to wait for a day or two, he would make her a set. On hearing this she was delighted, and fixed a date when she would collect them. The pipes were made and this lady came on the date arranged. She fondled them as if they were made of gold, and asked the price of them; but my father made a present of them to her. However, she insisted on paying and gave my father something for them. After some time my father and I happened to be at Hayling Island, when the lady made her appearance and, coming straight over to my father, she said, 'I am getting on very well with the

Pandeau pipes, I can play a tune or two.'

Now, I should like to say something about small or close-up magic, at which my father was especially adept. The first trick he taught me was the cups and balls, one of the earliest tricks known in magic. Briefly, it involves three metal cups, conical in shape, about four inches high and three inches in width, and three cork or sponge balls about an inch in diameter. These balls mysteriously passed from one cup to another, and finally five or six potatoes were left under them. The moves are executed during a running conversation, which is known as misdirection. One must learn to be natural in this class of entertainment, it is not always the quickness of the hand that deceives the eyes – far from it, since any quick movement might arouse suspicion. A classic example of this form of sleight-of-hand is known as the three-card trick, or Find the Lady, mostly used by swindlers to catch the unwary, though not so much in evidence today.

The operator would hold one card in the left hand, and two cards between the thumb, first and second fingers of the right hand, one being the Queen. The main deception was in the throw, the deft move by which the operator was able to throw down the Queen or an indifferent card at will.

In the days when train carriages had no corridors, four or five passengers were seated both sides. On Derby Day, trains were packed with people. The crook with a confederate, otherwise known as a 'Gee', would be seated in the centre. The crook would remark, 'Would any of you gentlemen like to see a card trick? Just a bit of entertainment?' Then he would spread a newspaper over his knees and produce a pack of cards, from which he selected three cards, including the Queen. He would then make a straight throw, so that the position of the Queen was obvious to anyone.

'Anyone know where the lady is?' the crook would ask. His 'Gee' would remark, 'That's easy, it's there', indicating the position of the Queen. 'And so it is', says the crook; 'if you had had a bet on this, you would have won. Let's have another throw.'

'I'll lay you a dollar that I can pick out the Queen,' his 'Gee' would say.

'All right then.'

Another straight throw by the crook, and the 'Gee' would win.

'Now wait a minute, let somebody else have a go,' remarked the crook. The passengers were certainly interested by now, and someone would have a go, for easy money, and the crook would purposely let him win.

Once the fever had caught on, the stakes were doubled and, when there was a considerable amount of money involved, the crook would execute the trick throw and scoop in the lot, saying 'Sorry you lost, gentlemen, but I had to take a sporting chance.'

Perhaps you would like to hear of another dodge that the unscrupulous conjurer used to get up to. This fellow and his confederate would enter a crowded public-house bar, and order a small beer or bitter. Then he would ask the landlord if he could show the customers a few tricks. Consent being given, and after a bit of by-play, this dishonest conjurer would ask the landlord if he would lend him a pound note for a trick, assuring the landlord that he would return it, and asking him to take the number of the pound note. This being done, and other customers noting the number, it was folded up and given to his confederate to hold. The confederate had a piece of paper folded to represent the note, and when the conjurer took back the pound note, a quick exchange was made undetected, and the confederate kept the pound note, whilst the conjurer had the piece of folded paper, which he placed inside an envelope, and proceeded to burn to the consternation of the landlord. Meanwhile the confederate quietly left the public bar and went to the saloon bar, calling for a small drink. The barmaid served him and he handed her the pound note, for which she gave him change, while the public bar were kept interested. The conjurer brought the trick to a climax by declaring that the pound note was in the till and, to the amazement of all, there it was, the barmaid had unconsciously placed it there. When the landlord checked up the till at night he discovered he was about nineteen shillings short, which he could not account for, the only reasonable conclusion being a mistake in change. I don't want my readers to get the idea that I took part in this sort of business, but being a conjurer I knew the dodges they used to get up to.

At last it was decided to dispose of the old van; it had done its work, and was getting beyond repair. Another private car was purchased. The rest of the summer season was spent visiting the various places. I worked up a good sailor trade. My mother looked after some of these boys and provided them with accommodation; they became great friends. A show was arranged at Lymington, near Bournemouth. It was a nasty wet night and on the return journey a car appeared in the distance. The driver must have been under the influence of drink, for it was driven in a most erratic manner. As it loomed up, I tried to get out of the way, but it came straight for me, and crash! my car was turned right over. How I escaped any injury is beyond me, but my father was knocked out. I managed to get him out, and Toby the dog was not hurt. Soon the police arrived and took down all particulars. Then an ambulance arrived, and took my father to Southampton Hospital, but he was not seriously injured, more or less suffering from shock.

I returned to Portsmouth by train with Toby. My wife was waiting for me, and guessed that something was wrong. I explained to her what had happened, and she said, 'Thank God, you are not hurt.'

The car was removed to a garage at Lyndhurst; it was completely wrecked and beyond repair. My father was soon released from hospital, and completely recovered. After some legal proceedings, a settlement in my favour was made, but I was without a car. My Uncle Jack wanted my father and me to perform a Punch and Judy Show at a fête in Oxford in aid of the Morris football team.

I went to the garage where I parked the last car to see if the proprietor had one for hire. He said that one was for sale, and if I was going to Oxford I could try it out. It was a Morris Cowley, very roomy, but I could see it had plenty of wear. However, I accepted his offer.

My mother and some sailor friends decided to come with my father and me to Oxford in the car. After I had been driving for a while I heard a slight knocking sound, apparently coming from the rear, but which I did not take much notice of; but on leaving Sutton Scotney, it became much louder, so I stopped and said, 'All get out; there's a knocking sound at the back.' I jacked the car up at the back and in those days the wheels were made with spokes, covered by sheet metal, and when I removed the nuts holding it, the centre of the wheel fell out. The nuts must have worked loose and vibration through continual running was the cause of the trouble. I had a spare wheel; the other I chucked over the hedge, and we reached Oxford without further trouble.

They all had an enjoyable day, and I returned to Portsmouth without any bother. As the car did not meet with my satisfaction, I did not buy it.

My father had an accident, injuring his back, and it was some time before he recovered; meanwhile I attended the shows on my own. I remember on one occasion I had an engagement at a wedding party, to do conjuring and ventriloquism. It was a lively party and the drinks were freely passed round, and they would include me. Having finished the entertainment I packed up quickly, unaware that the legs of the ventriloquial figure were protruding from the case. I was walking along the road towards the Gosport Ferry when a policeman came from behind and stopped me, and said, 'I have been following you for some time. What have you got in that case?' I soon discovered the reason for his suspicion, and as I was in a merry mood, as one can imagine, I replied, 'Oh! the body is inside.' With this he got quite nasty and barked out, 'Open that case.' I did so and took the figure out exclaiming, 'That's the body, a ventriloquial doll!' After he had a look at it, he said, 'You understand, I got to do my duty', or words to that effect, and walked away.

After a while it was decided to put the pub on the market, and take over a restaurant near by. It was a very busy restaurant, but my father became very ill, through the injury he had to the back, and died in 1935. This left my mother and me to run the restaurant with the help of my wife. It was very old property, and a demolition order was issued for it, after which my mother went into private business and catered for boarders.

Chapter 10

*My second meeting with Captain Kettle; the bottler; I carve
a set of Punch and Judy figures; Charlie comes to the fairground; hypnotism with a coloured man; I lose and find
Toby; I join the forces again*

My wife and I took over a small shop in Queen Street,
Portsmouth, more or less for accommodation for the time
being. I was walking along Arundel Street when I came
across a small shop with some conjuring apparatus in the
window. I went inside and, to my surprise, who was
behind the counter? None other than Captain Kettle. He
was by now getting on in years, but for his age he was
still very active. He looked at me and then, suddenly, it
dawned on him who I was and he exclaimed, 'Why, it's
Vic Taylor!' I shook hands with him and told him that I
had lost my father. He apparently was down on his luck,
and was struggling to make a living, and asked me what I
was doing. I said, 'At the moment nothing, but if I could
get someone to bottle for me I would take the Punch and
Judy Show to Hayling Island and various other places.'
On hearing this he immediately offered to do the bottling.

I bought a small Morris van and once more got to work
with the Punch and Judy Show. Now the bottler (collector) had fourpence in the shilling as his share of the
takings. A good bottler was worth his corner, as there was

an art in collecting. One might think anyone could go round with a bag, but this is not so. In the first place one has to be courteous in such a manner as not to take no for an answer. The bottler would start collecting on the outside of the crowd first, as these people would move off quicker than those in front. A continual watch was kept for fresh comers, and as soon as they saw a bit of the show the bottler would approach them with the bag. Some would say, 'I've only just come up.' Then the collector would exclaim, 'Oh! Yes, but could I have your donation now. It will save me coming to you again', or words to that effect. Towards the end of the show the bottler would collect in the centre and front of the crowd. Captain Kettle had all these qualities, so I went dead halves with him in the takings. Sometimes, a showman would get a bad bottler, who would be dishonest, and help himself to the takings. This in those days was called 'palling' or 'hot rolling'; this, of course, was a serious crime. The performer would know how much a pitch ought to realize; and if the takings continued to be poor on the pitches, the performer would know that the bottler was 'palling' him. It was one day at Hayling Island; I had just finished a show when a lady approached me and said, 'My son has seen your show, and he is going in for it, and says what lovely figures you have. Do you know where I could buy them?' I replied, 'Nowhere! I make my own.' Which was true. I carved all my own figures. She said, 'I wish you would carve my son a set.' This was arranged and I carved the figures and my wife dressed them. Her son was about fifteen or sixteen years old, and he used to watch my show continually until he had every word of the dialogue pat. I instructed him in the art of the Punch and Judy Show, and later on he became a professional. To my knowledge he has had those figures for thirty years and is still using them.

At the end of the season Captain Kettle got hold of a dockyard man who was mad about conjuring. The fair on Portsdown Hill was arriving shortly and Captain Kettle wanted to have a side-show of the illusion of 'The Human Spider' there. He promised this dockyard man that he would be able to display his skill as a conjurer on the show, but some cash was needed to put the proposition into action; so enthusiastic was the dockyard man that he consented to finance the whole issue.

Captain Kettle asked me to come in with him. I wasn't keen on fair work, but eventually I consented. The booth or tent, proscenium, lighting and other props were acquired, the fair arrived and the dockyard man (who became known as Charlie), Kettle and I built the show up on the allotted site. Charlie, instead of putting on a false moustache, painted one with grease paint which looked like a black blob below his nose.

This was done so that he would not be recognized, but this wasn't sufficient. Charlie, Kettle and I were out in front of the show doing our stuff, and amongst the crowd were some of Charlie's dockyard mates who saw through his disguise, and shouted out, 'There's old Charlie! Wotcher, Charlie, what's that underneath yer nose.' So embarrassed was Charlie that he disappeared inside the show.

I was glad when the fair finished, as I have already remarked that I didn't care for fair work. I often saw Charlie afterwards and had many a chat with him, mainly about magic. Captain Kettle helped me in the ensuing private shows, which he was glad to do.

It so happened one day that some old colonel walked into Captain Kettle's shop and wanted some instruction in hypnotism. Captain Kettle explained that he was a very busy man, which he would have liked to be, just a bit of showmanship to impress the customer. However, a date was arranged for a demonstration and a course of so many lessons; but Captain Kettle insisted on a deposit, which the old boy readily paid; meanwhile Captain Kettle procured the services of a coloured man to act as a subject. On the date arranged the old boy was there, and the coloured man sat in a chair. After some preparation, which was quite unnecessary, Captain Kettle got the coloured man to gaze at a disc, and started to make some form of hypnotic passes in front of him; but the coloured man was slow to respond. Suddenly the old boy produced a pin and plunged it into the subject's fleshy part of the posterior. Immediately the coloured man, with a yelp, leapt out of the chair and ran out of the shop. The old boy thought it a swindle and walked out.

Another summer season came along and the usual call was made at my father-in-law's small pub; after a drink, we proceeded to Hayling Island, which was about five miles farther on. At the end of the day's work with Punch and Judy, Toby the dog was missing, probably lured away by someone with ice cream, which it was very fond of. Captain Kettle and I searched everywhere but without success. I slowly drove along the road, with the idea that Toby thought I had gone off without her, and that I might pick her up on the road, but there was no sign of her. I was much distressed and inserted an advert in the paper, before going to Hayling Island again the next day. Calling at my father-in-law's pub, I said I had lost Toby. He just smiled and at that moment Toby ran into the bar and was all over me. She had covered the five miles from Hayling to Havant, and knowing the pub barked until she was let in. But wasn't I relieved to get Toby back again? How she became missing was a mystery; if only a dog could speak.

Towards 1939 a war with Germany seemed inevitable, and it reminded me that I had at some time or other signed a paper holding me down on the R.A.F. reserve. It was so long ago that I never really gave it a thought, being so actively engaged in other pursuits. A general mobilization took place, and I received a notice to the effect that I was on a class 'E' reserve, and would I report to Fort Grange, Gosport. I thought it was only a matter of reporting, and said as much to my wife; but on my arrival there, I found a crowd of men on the same reserve as myself, mostly of middle age and up to sixty.

After a medical examination, I was sent over to an improvised equipment stores. The uniforms were in cardboard boxes, with the individual's name on; the sizes of the uniforms were taken from measurements of previous service. I was requested to take the uniform intended for me from the box and put it on. My civilian clothes were packed in the same box and sent to my home address. Fortunately, I had not altered much and to some degree my uniform fitted me, but others had so changed during the gap of their previous service that they couldn't get the tunics together owing to the weight they had put on, whilst others had gone thin and the tunics hung like sacks on them, not to mention the trousers. A more motley crowd one can't imagine. The Station Warrant Officer started to call out names for posting. When it came to my turn I had the greatest luck in the world: I was posted to Thorney Island, near Portsmouth.

Chapter 11

I am called up for service; the concert party; my home is bombed at Portsmouth; my wife goes to Havant; I do shows for Dr Barnardo's Homes; I help to build Thorney Island theatre; I meet with an old friend at the Grand Theatre, Brighton; experiences in Northern Ireland; the I.R.A.; war ends and I get discharged from the R.A.F.

On my way to Thorney Island, I called home; my wife wondered what had happened to me, and was more surprised to see me in uniform, for I had been absent for three or four days. I explained to her what had happened, and that I was on my way to Thorney Island.

On my arrival at Thorney Island, I found other men just arrived on the same reserve, and friendship was established right away. It was glorious weather and for about a fortnight it was a proper holiday. Then war broke out between Britain and Germany on 3 September 1939. For a few months nothing happened, then the Germans broke through the French and British lines, and with the capitulation of France, the evacuation of Dunkirk followed. Every ship, large and small, was used to evacuate the British troops from the French coast. It was a gigantic and glorious achievement, but as most people know this history I won't dwell on it any further.

Apart from my work in the R.A.F. I tried to establish a concert party. I got together anyone willing to do a turn, a show was arranged with the permission of the Station Warrant Officer (after this I shall refer to him as the S.W.O.) in the canteen. So successful was this impromptu entertainment that I was requested to get up another one. This was arranged, and it went off even better than the first one. From the talent I had collected, this formed the foundation of a permanent concert party. The acting entertainments officer took over the party and from then on rehearsing began in real earnest. Owing to the incessant air-raids over Portsmouth, my wife took to sleeping at her people's pub at Havant. I did not give up the place in Queen Street; after all, it was home; but one day, my wife went to Portsmouth and found it had had a direct hit with a bomb, and all that was left was a crater; so that was the end of my home in Portsmouth; I procured a sleeping-out pass, and stayed at the pub; anyway, it was nearer to Thorney Island.

A certain lady who was connected with Dr Barnardo's Homes often phoned the Group Captain to let me off to do shows in aid of these homes; the lady in question was such an erratic driver that sometimes I was scared stiff. My wife used to accompany me on these shows. One very wet night she nearly got to Rustington, Sussex, where the performance was to be held, when her car went wrong. With the help of another person, the car was pushed into Rustington, and at the side of the hall was a very muddy patch of ground. Whilst I was pushing on this muddy patch I fell over; as I was in dress suit, you can imagine what a state I was in; however, I managed to wipe some mud off, and rinsed my hands. I did not feel much like

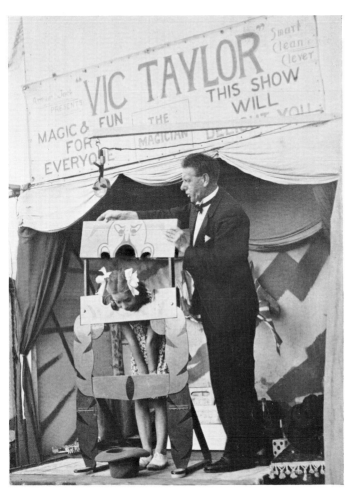

Performing on Southsea beach in the summer of 1946

Three old performers in semi-retirement

doing a show, but I went through with it. By this time a mechanic had put her car right and, leaving Rustington, she lost her way and must have travelled round in circles until the Home Guard suddenly appeared and stopped the car. After some questions, they put her on the right road, and my wife and I arrived at Havant in the early hours of the morning.

The Thorney concert party became well known, and throughout the air-raids we did performances in various places. Fortunately the party escaped the bombs. Another entertainments officer replaced the former one, and he was all out to further the efforts of the concert party; so much so that he had the idea of transforming a transport hangar into a theatre and cinema. One day the S.W.O. called me to the office and said 'You know all about theatres?' I replied, 'It was in my line.' Then the S.W.O. said, 'Under the Entertainments Officer, I want you to take charge of transforming the old transport hangar into a theatre and cinema. You will have plenty of helpers.'

This was a bigger job than I bargained for. Down the centre were about four large brick pillars, supporting the roof; these would certainly have to be removed for a start. The entertainments officer arranged for this to be done, but before they could be removed, steel tubular stanchions on either side, with girders running across, had to be erected, to support the roof when the brick pillars were removed. It took some time before these could be supplied; eventually this was completed.

The entertainments officer kept me well employed collecting anything useful off blitz sites; then he arranged for seats from two blitzed cinemas. I had a host of fellows with screw-drivers, fixing them together; the dressing-rooms, stage and lighting were completed by tradesmen on the camp; the hangar had sliding doors, and these could be opened in a few seconds in case of fire. After weeks of hard work the Thorney theatre and cinema was established, which is still in existence to this very day.

A band of professional musicians from Uxbridge was posted to Thorney and David Burnaby from the Co-optimists was lent to organize entertainment; also a professional actor played a big part in producing shows which were equal, if not better, than some of the shows outside. On one occasion a broadcast of a production was made entitled *Mr Smith* and on another occasion the 'Windmill Girls under Van Damm, the proprietor and manager of the Windmill Theatre, London', paid a visit to Thorney theatre.

The band and a few turns including myself were to appear at the Grand Theatre, Brighton. This brought back memories to me as being about the last theatre I played in. Arriving there by train, as other transport wasn't available, at the theatre the old baggage man was still there, 'Old Thomas'. After all those years he recognized me, and greeted me like a long-lost brother. This called for a drink up at the local and after the show he would insist on carrying my case to the station, and his last words were, 'You will look after my old friend, won't you?'

One of the finest shows produced at the Thorney Theatre was a pantomime, *Cinderella*. After weeks of rehearsal and preparation, no professional show could equal it; this was put on at the South Parade Pier, Southsea, and played to a full house. E.N.S.A. shows came regularly to Thorney, but suddenly the entertainments officer was posted. I continued for a while in charge of the theatre, and then I was posted to various stations in the country.

Then I returned to Thorney Island, but I did not stay very long, before I was posted to Kiladeas, near Enniskillen, Northern Ireland. It was a small camp, on the shores of Loch Erne. Whilst I was there, I met a script writer, and it was decided to try to get a concert party together. I found out the entertainments officer and he was all for it. Being a small camp it was difficult to find enough talent, but eventually I managed to get hold of one or two W.R.A.F.s who could sing a song, and some fellows who offered to do some sort of a turn, and so rehearsing took place. The great difficulty was getting hold of someone to play the piano; at last I found a fellow who could play moderately and, although not on the scale of Thorney Island, after a while a fairly presentable concert party took shape.

I built three illusions whilst I was there: an empty box to produce a person, the 'artist's dream', but the greatest one was a levitation, 'The floating and vanishing lady'. This last illusion took three persons to work it, but it was so rehearsed that everything was done to a split second. One fellow, who came into the party, asked me if I was doing the razor blade trick. I replied that I wasn't and asked him why? He said, 'Cos, I eats 'em.' His turn was

[89]

bending six-inch nails with bare hands, lying on a board with bare back, with large nails driven through and various other feats of strength.

With the aid of Bert, the script writer, the concert party improved so much that the entertainments officer was able to take the party to other camps and various places around. The concert hall at the camp was small, but it suited the purpose of the personnel on the camp. An airman came to me and expressed his desire to join the concert party; on asking what he could do he replied, 'I am a magician.' I replied, 'I am too!'

On witnessing his turn he had some very good tricks, including a watch trick, but he certainly did not know how to put them over. I thought that I could use him at some time or the other, so I gave him some instruction which he was very pleased to follow. A show was arranged for the camp, and as I had already been on the bill on several occasions, I thought I would put this chappie on the programme. On the night of the show he was very nervous, but I assured him that there was nothing to be nervous about. He did his tricks very well until he wanted to borrow a watch. Who should lend him one but the Group Captain. On returning to the stage, he dropped it. Although the idea was to smash it up, and produce it elsewhere, he thought that he really had damaged the real watch, and terminated the trick as quickly as possible. I was in the dressing-room with him when the Group Captain stalked in saying, 'Whatever have you done to my watch?'

The airman stammered out, 'Is it all right, sir?'

The Group Captain replied, 'All right? I should think it is. It hasn't been going for a long time, and now it is.'

The concert party was to appear at the British Legion, Enniskillen; the stage consisted of some planks on trestles. The opening chorus of W.R.A.F.s went on, and during their dancing number the planks tipped up at one end; what a commotion! The W.R.A.F.s all slid on their backsides on top of each other; this caused the biggest laugh of the evening; at first the entertainments officer was in a flat spin, but even he saw the funny side of it afterwards.

Another show was arranged by the entertainments officer for a certain lady in aid of some funds. The place where the performance had to take place was right on the border and a long journey from the camp. The coach was within two miles of the place when it was stopped and two Ulster policemen armed with revolvers boarded it. They said it was necessary to stand by in case of trouble.

On arriving at the hall it was quite evident that the Southern Irishman was intent on causing trouble. Before the show commenced there was a hell of a row, jeering, booing, catcalls, to such extent that the Ulster policemen had their hands on the revolvers at the ready. It was hopeless for the party to make a start; however, I suggested that an Irish W.R.A.F., who had no fear, should go and sing some Southern Irish songs. The entertainments officer was very reluctant about this, but at last he consented, and so amidst the row this Irish lass opened up with some Irish songs. Gradually the din died down and they started singing. She was kept on until it was all quiet and the rest of the show was well received; but this Irish lass definitely saved the situation.

After the entertainment a dance took place, in which some of our fellows joined in. The entertainments officer ordered me to get the men out when it was time the party left. I went in the hall and asked an Irishman how long a certain dance would last. 'All night,' replied the Irishman. At last I got them out but, before the coach could move off, the Irish women loaded the party with cakes large and small and other commodities, thus a good send-off. The Ulster police left the coach at their post saying, 'You were lucky. That was a near thing.'

A few more miles on the journey back the party was ambushed by the I.R.A. Everyone was ordered out and lined up. After looking at the identification cards, and making a search, they ordered the party back on the coach, and to get on their way. As no harm was done it wasn't reported.

Some time before D-Day, Enniskillen and other parts of Northern Ireland were full of Americans, and for about nine months no one was allowed to leave or enter Northern Ireland. Suddenly in one night every American had disappeared; security had done its job, and so the invasion of France had begun. The concert party did several shows, but gradually faded out, as they were wanted for other duties. On 8 May 1945 Germany surrendered unconditionally and on 15 August 1945 Japan surrendered unconditionally. I was discharged from the R.A.F. soon afterwards.

Chapter 12

Street shows; a chap named Bunk; cinema club shows; last of a school show; Punch and Judy; other shows, including meeting with Earl Jellicoe; on the cinema screen; I take over the pub at Ryde; Christmas Day, I lose and recover my dress coat and vest; on board the H.M.S. 'Implacable'

To celebrate victory nearly everyone organized street shows for the children; this consisted of tables the length of the street at which the children sat down to a good feed of tea, sandwiches and cakes. At the time I was in great demand to perform Punch and Judy Shows at these parties, and I did good business going from one street to another. The only trouble was transport, as not many cars were manufactured during the war, except for military use; so if I hired a taxi, some old crock that had seen its last days would appear, and I was not sure of always getting to my destination. However, I solved this problem by purchasing an old 1930 Austin 7; it was a rough arrangement, but the engine was particularly good.

At one of these shows, I met a chap who used to busk around the pubs, prior to the war. He only knew one song that was, 'Bunky doodle lido, follow the Sergeant Major', and with a couple of grunts on the concertina this was sufficient for a collection. To my surprise, old 'Bunk' (the name he went by) had a line of children marching behind him, and he was playing the accordion in a professional manner.

I greeted him with, 'Hello, Bunk, you've come up in the world.'

He said, 'I got a job in the dockyard during the war, and I learnt to play the accordion properly.'

'Good for you!' I replied.

My wife now helped me in the shows and the little Austin acted beautifully. For some time the street parties were in full swing. The cinemas gave a morning children's club show at which I was engaged to perform Punch and Judy, and I played every cinema in Portsmouth. Long queues of children formed outside the cinemas chanting, 'We want the Punch and Judy.' This went on for some time, until for some reason or the other it faded out.

Ever since the war ended, year after year, I performed for the infants at a certain school in a poor locality of Portsmouth, and the children did enjoy my entertainment. The headmistress used to say, 'See you next year.' I wrote to this headmistress one year, which I always did to keep a date open for them, and she replied with the news that other arrangements had been made, and that she was no longer headmistress. It came under the senior department and no fund was allowed for the entertainment, but rather than disappoint the children, as they looked forward to my visit so, she said she would pay my fee out of her own pocket, and that was the last performance.

I was once engaged to do a Punch and Judy Show at

Chidham, not far from Havant; it was at a big house in the village; there were some elderly people there and I asked the lady responsible where the children were. She said, 'Oh! there's no children, the idea is to go back to our younger days, when we watched the Punch and Judy Show on the beach.' And they thoroughly enjoyed the show.

Punch and Judy is a very old show and I am afraid that many performers of it have passed beyond. It is a glove puppet entertainment which apparently originated from the East. Puppet entertainments then became popular in Europe. In Italy the script was based on a real-life drama known as *Pulchinello*. Pulchinello was a hunchback who cared nothing for law or order; he beat his wife to death, knocked a policeman about, chucked the baby out of the window; in all, he was a downright villain. In my show, I cut out most of the grim material in the original script. This type of performance travelled through France known as *Punchinello*, and eventually came to Britain, and was entitled 'Punch and Judy'. It is really a Royal Show, for some old king – I cannot name the king – gave it a Royal Charter to be performed any time in any side-street for twenty minutes, without interference and this act has never been repealed.

I use fifteen figures in my show, of which the heads and hands are attached to the dress. The heads have a round hole bored in them, for the insertion of the fore-finger; the thumb and other fingers are inside the sleeves of the dress. Sewn on the end of the dresses are straight hooks, and the figures are hung upside down on a rope

[95]

stretched between the framework of the show. This enables the performer to dive his hand into the dress, and produce the figure he needs.

In the earlier pages of this book, I have described the squeaky voice of Punch, known to old-time performers as the 'swatchel', or 'call'. In presenting the show, the performer has to bring these figures to life by plenty of movement and impersonating voice and manner of the figure he is portraying. It is a very difficult show to learn, since old-time performers were very reluctant to give tips to a beginner without payment.

I knew an old Punch and Judy showman who used to perform on Southsea beach before the First World War. His show was somewhat dilapidated, but he was a very fine performer, if very partial to 'booze'. He was engaged to do a show on one of the ships in the Dockyard; to confirm the engagement, he was given half the fee, the worst thing that could have happened. The Punch and Judy set up was not collapsible, but a fixture, and it was conveyed to different places on a couple of wheels. The time arrived for the party, but the old showman hadn't turned up; the skipper was getting anxious so he sent a couple of sailors out to find him. In one of the streets in Old Portsmouth, they saw his show standing outside a pub, so they went in and found the old showman 'flaked out' on a seat. All they could do was to carry him out, throw him in the show and wheel them both to the Dockyard. Between the two of them, they managed to haul him up the gangway. The skipper was furious and burst out in no uncertain language: 'Why, the man is dead drunk!

Take him down below and revive him.' They managed to do this, and revive him they did, whatever they gave him must have been pretty strong, for he 'came to' and did the show.

On one occasion I had an engagement of magic and ventriloquism to do for Earl Jellicoe, late Admiral of the fleet, at St Lawrence, near Ryde, Isle of Wight. It was a winter's night, the snow lay on the ground, and Earl Jellicoe's chauffeur met me at Ryde. Earl Jellicoe was the perfect gentleman. After the show, which the children thoroughly enjoyed, he showed me a silver model of the flagship *The Iron Duke*, which his crew had presented to him on his retirement from the Navy.

As my props increased, the Austin car was too small to accommodate them, so I procured a 1934 Morris van. I did not have much trouble with her, and on the whole it was a good buy. Before and after the Second World War, I did the children's parties at the H.M.S. *Dolphin* submarine depot. On one particular occasion, the officer in charge said to me, 'We are taking a film of the Punch and Judy Show.' I naturally thought it was just someone interested with a cine-camera. With that I never gave it another thought. Suddenly the film people burst into the place, erected their equipment and turned the place into a blaze of light, and asked me to give them a cue for the best part of my show. I was somewhat unprepared for this. However, I complied with their request. The manager of the Havant cinema was a great friend of mine, being a magician, and I told him what had occurred. He said, 'I've been waiting for you to turn up. Your show is in News

[97]

Flash. Want to see it?' I replied, 'Indeed, I do', so I saw my own show on the screen.

I took a stand on the children's playground, Southsea, and for a time my wife did the bottling.

My wife's parents were getting advanced in age, and they asked me if I would like to take over the pub. Well, really, I had no choice at the time, and so I became the landlord of the pub. It wasn't doing much trade, and I was forced to continue in the show line.

I came in contact with an old-time comedian; he proved to be a good bottler. With his help a shelter to accommodate about a hundred people was erected in case it rained. I had this stand for about three years; each year the price of the stand increased. At last I considered it was not worth it, so I relied on private engagements. For a number of years I performed at Ryde carnival. As it was too expensive to convey the van over by the ferry, a man and his wife helped with the props; not only was it remunerative, it was also a day out for them. My wife could no longer accompany me on the shows, as she was looking after the pub and attending to her parents. The trouble with the carnival was that the ground was some distance away from Ryde pier, and the secretary of the show used to send all sorts of transport for me. On one occasion a pantechnicon drew up at Ryde pier; the driver was certainly looking for someone. At last I said, 'You're not looking for me by any chance?'

'I am looking for someone with a load of stuff to take to the ground.'

I said, 'That's me. I am the Punch and Judy man.'

He replied, 'Is that all you got?'

It was quite evident the secretary had not told him who I was, and he expected a load of furniture or suchlike. Anyhow, he conveyed the props to the ground, saying, 'I wouldn't have brought this bloody thing out if I had known.'

Eventually I informed the secretary that I was booked up one year. I was glad to free myself from this engagement, as it entailed so much hard work.

Through an agent, I had a booking one Christmas Day with Punch and Judy on one of the small ships in the Dockyard. A friend of mine out of the R.A.F. accompanied me. On arriving at this particular ship, the officer in charge said, 'Hello, you are the Punch and Judy man; we also have a magician coming.'

I replied, 'I didn't know you had a magician coming.'

It appears that this agent only booked me to do Punch and Judy, and overlooked the fact that I was wanted for conjuring as well.

The officer in charge asked me if I did conjuring. I replied that I did. He said, 'If I get a fast car your friend could get your props, it's only to Havant, it wouldn't take five minutes.'

I replied that it would take a bit longer than that. However, the car arrived and I said to my friend, 'My wife will know what I require and ask her to put my vest and dress jacket in.'

Meanwhile I built up and did the Punch and Judy Show. My friend arrived back with the necessary props. In the hurry the vest and dress jacket were put on the back seat and before my friend could clamber up the iron gangway, the car went off with them. However, I did the conjuring show, and then I explained to the officer what had occurred. He said, 'That's all right, my friend will be back in a minute with the car, make yourselves comfortable in the Ward Room.' With that he plonked a bottle of whisky down on the table, and left.

My friend and I had consumed about half the whisky when the officer looked in and said, 'You chaps all right? He won't be long now.' I replied that my friend and I were quite all right!

My friend and I finished up the bottle of whisky; after all it was Christmas Day, why not celebrate? The officer did not put in another appearance, and neither did the car, and I thought it was time to make some inquiry. I found a Chief Petty Officer who happened to be the jaunty, and explained to him that if a car turned up and left a vest and dress jacket with him, would he send it to my Havant address, and that I would pay all expenses, or I would call for them. It was some time after the Christmas holiday, and I heard no more about the missing garments, so I decided to go to the agent in Portsmouth and collect my fee. On seeing him he said, 'Some silly clot of a sailor left part of a dress suit here.' I informed him that it happened to be mine; he was somewhat surprised, until I explained the circumstances, so I don't know who was the clot, him or the sailor.

I performed on quite a number of ships of the Royal Navy; on one, H.M.S. *Implacable*, aircraft carrier, my wife arranged to come with me. I had amplifying gear in the van which I used for the Punch and Judy; also I had to use a twelve-volt accumulator which, of course, was fairly heavy. I went up the gangway and saw the duty officer and asked him for a couple of ratings to help me with the gear. Suddenly a swarm of sailors appeared, enough to shift the British Navy, let alone my bit of gear.

It was towards evening time when I finished my show, and most of the sailors had gone ashore and I was wondering how I was going to get my gear to the van, when a few sailors lined up. The jaunty was about to dismiss them, but I rushed up and asked for some help. The jaunty pointed to some and said, 'You, you, you, shift this chap's gear,' and dismissed the rest.

I said to my wife, 'I want to get hold of the secretary the settle for the show, you get down to the van.' Then I realized that I seemed to be alone in this vast space below decks, until I saw a shadowy figure, which proved to be a sailor. I asked him if he could take me to the secretary. He said, 'I'm just off, but if you go through this passage and that passage, you'll find the place.' I tried to follow his directions until I saw some other chap and he took me along a maze of passages. I was properly bewildered. The secretary wasn't in his abode, and this chap and I went from one place to another. I wished that I had never attempted to find the secretary. It was like looking for a pin in a haystack.

At last this chap and I went through a door, and came across the skipper addressing all the big noises and their wives. The skipper turned round and said, 'Hello, where did you bob from?' The secretary happened to be there, and I said, 'I have business with the secretary.' On hearing this he ordered the secretary to take me below and get it over.

I came down a gangway at the other end of the ship. My wife was waiting with the van, and said, 'Wherever have you been?' I explained to her what had happened, and she said, 'I shouldn't accept any more engagements on ships.'

But I did and it happened to be the H.M.S. *Implacable* again. It was a fine summer's day and I had built up the Punch and Judy Show next to the superstructure of the flight deck of the *Implacable*; part of the deck was roped off. On the superstructure were several men in overalls, smoking and relaxing in general, when I saw one coming our way, a little man with a bald pate, followed by a group of people. It suddenly flashed across my mind it was Prime Minister Attlee. I said to my friend, 'Here comes Attlee.' Suddenly the foreman came rushing up shouting, 'Put those fags out and get busy. Here comes the Prime Minister.' They sprang into action wielding paint brushes in all directions until the Prime Minister had passed. This time I did not have any trouble collecting my fee, the secretary sought me out and paid me before the show was over.

Towards the winter I let the show work, rest, owing to the fact that my mother became very ill, and after lingering for a long time she passed away in 1959, so I lost the best parents a son could possibly have. My wife lost her parents soon afterwards.

Chapter 13

*Two half-crowns and the inspector; the Ascot Gold Cup;
winter 1963 and a journey to Gosport; what happened in
the hall; the show at Southwick; a blunder and success;
children's entertainment; a recollection of old-time performers*

I did not pursue show business until I got things squared
up. I had two trick half-crowns. I was meddling about
with them one morning; they could not be told from the
genuine ones, unless handled and subjected to a close
examination. For some reason I left them on the dresser,
and my wife promptly paid the milkman with them.

I said, 'Where's those half-crowns?'

My wife replied, 'I did not know. I paid the milkman
with them.'

'Oh Lord, those were trick ones; I can't get them replaced,' I said.

The chances of recovering them seemed to be out of
the question. I phoned the proprietor of the milk firm,
asking him if he could check up any money he had in, as
two unusual half-crowns might be amongst it. This he
kindly did, but without any results. My wife went into a
greengrocer's shop, just above, run by a woman, and she
said to my wife, 'You be careful, there's some dud half-
crowns around, I have had two passed to me.' My wife
asked her what she had done with them.

She said, 'I gave them to the baker, and he is taking them to the police station!'

When my wife told me this, I went to the shop and inquired when the baker would be round again. I was informed that he would be around in the afternoon. I waited for him to appear. After a while the baker came along with his van. I immediately stopped him and asked him if he had had two dud half-crowns handed to him.

He said, 'Yes! How did you know?'

I gave him an explanation of what had occurred, and asked what he had done with them.

He replied, 'Well, they wasn't any good to me and as I was near the police station I handed them in!' So I went to the police station and inquired about them. The policeman on duty said, 'The inspector would like to see you.'

I knocked on his door.

'Come in, Mr Taylor! I have been expecting you to claim your property, and I know you are a conjurer, and how ingenious these coins are. Could you get me a couple made like them?' said the Inspector.

I thanked him and collected the half-crowns and promised to try to procure a couple of trick coins for him, but I knew this was hopeless.

Whilst on the subject of coins, I did a coin trick with a matchbox, six pennies and a dice, although it took considerable dexterity of sleight-of-hand. I never really attached any importance to it until, by chance, I provided it with a name and a story. It then became the most popular trick in my repertoire, and it came about in this way.

An elderly gentleman, a sort of farmer – indeed, he dressed like one – used my pub regularly. He also cultivated watercress of the finest quality, which he sent all over the country. This gentleman was very interested in boxing, and in his younger days often had a bout in the boxing booths in the fairs. He used to enjoy a chat with me, because I could converse upon this subject.

One day he said, 'Vic, you remember when the Ascot Gold Cup was stolen.'

I replied that I remembered the incident.

'Do you know how it was got away?' he continued.

I said, 'No! how was it got away?'

'Well,' he said, 'I was at the death-bed of an old friend who was involved in the robbery and he said, "Harry! I might as well tell you it was got away under a wagon-load of hay." '

I simply said, 'How interesting!'

I was displaying the trick which I have mentioned above when the story of the Ascot Gold Cup came into my mind. I showed the dice, and told the story how the Ascot Gold Cup was stolen, and that the dice represented the Cup, and furthermore six coppers were sent down to guard it, this being the six penny pieces. I then covered the dice with the matchbox, and this was covered with a glass. The six policemen went in various directions, leaving one policeman to guard the Gold Cup, who eventually fell asleep. The coppers were vanished one by one by means of sleight-of-hand, and the robbers got busy. I then removed the glass and matchbox: the dice had disappeared and in its place were the six pennies. After a bit of patter about how the policemen were puzzled, I touched one of the onlookers on the head and produced the coins from his nose and, removing the matchbox, revealed the dice, and said, 'And so the Gold Cup was recovered.' Of course, this was an alteration in the original story.

It became so well known that I was requested to perform the Ascot Gold Cup countless times, so much so that I became bored doing the trick.

Another coin trick I performed was called the aerial mint, in which I produced half-crowns from the air, and various other places and dropped them into a tin.

At one show, I included this in the programme. After the entertainment, the gentleman responsible was about to pay me when he remarked in a joke, 'Why should I pay you your fee; you must be a rich man to produce money when you like.' He then settled my bill.

It was during that terrible winter of 1963 that I was engaged to do a three-hour performance of Punch and Judy, conjuring, ventriloquism and marionettes at Gosport. I had a very good assistant at the time, and after a tedious journey through snow and ice, arrived at the Hall. I had electrical equipment especially for the marionettes to fix up; the nearest point my assistant could connect to was a shaky old power point.

I went through the show without a hitch; the marionette show was the last item on the programme, which I had just finished and bid the audience good-night. I said to my assistant, 'Well, that's over, unplug the juice.'

He certainly did; my electrical equipment was in good order, but apparently the old power point wasn't; not only did my assistant receive a violent shock, but the whole place was plunged into darkness.

The old caretaker had no idea where the fuse-boxes were situated, my assistant and I groped around with a torch, but without success and, as it was getting late, I decided to pack up with the light of the torch. I bundled the props in the van anyhow and started the journey back to Havant. It was terrible. I could only engage a low gear and, even so, I was skidding from one ice rut to another; there were cars stranded all along the road.

After what seemed an endless journey, I reached Havant in one piece, although my nerves were a bit on edge; a couple of stiff brandies for my assistant and myself soon put this right.

I remember at a show that was booked for a pub known as the Red Lion at Southwick on Portsdown Hill I had trouble with the van. I was almost outside the pub when for no reason at all the van suddenly conked out, right in the centre of the road; a naval coach pulled up, and in no uncertain language the driver shouted out to me to get out of it. I was in no mood to be spoken to in this way, and I shouted back, 'You don't think that I have stopped here for fun; if you were anything like, you would help me off the road.' With this he said no more.

My assistant and I pushed the van on to a green patch which was an usual uphill; on the other side were a few houses, then a door opened and a woman appeared shouting, 'You can't stop here!'

I shouted back, 'What do you mean, I can't stop here? I am not interfering with you, or obstructing your view.'

Again she bellowed, 'You can't stop here!'

At last I told her to shut her trap up; with this she nearly went into hysterics, shouting: 'I'll tell my husband', and went inside, slamming the door. After lugging the cases to the pub, my assistant and I had a couple of drinks to cool off.

The show was in a hut just outside, which was successfully accomplished and, with the aid of a few willing helpers, the van was given a push and away she went.

It is not unusual at some time or other a magician may slip up and I am no exception to the rule, but an experienced performer will cover up the mistake the best way possible and the audience are no wiser, no matter how weak the ending; and on one occasion this happened to me. I was performing a trick in which a borrowed handkerchief was torn up, restored, mutilated, burnt and so on; eventually it was recovered from the smallest box of a nest of boxes. The result depended on the assistant obtaining the handkerchief from the performer by secret means, and placing it in the smallest box of the nest.

I don't know what happened to my assistant, but he missed his cue and I was left with the handkerchief that I had planted. During the presentation of the trick, I realized a mistake had been made. I quickly recovered the handkerchief from its hiding place, and slipped it into my pocket. My assistant was making all sorts of frantic signs to me, but it was too late, and I was thinking of a way out to end the trick satisfactorily.

During the performance I was pestered by a fellow who was making a confounded nuisance of himself by telling those around him how the tricks were done. He pointed to the boxes and said, 'You see, he will get the handkerchief out of the smallest one.'

I knew differently, and actually he was playing right into my hands. I took out all the boxes until I came to the smallest one, and I said, 'For the benefit of that gentleman, the handkerchief is *not* in the box as he suggests', and I opened the box and showed it empty. 'But,' I said, 'it is in my pocket!' and I produced the handkerchief to a thunderous round of applause. The fellow was crestfallen, and shut up like a book, and I had no more trouble from him during the remainder of the entertainment, and that is how I turned a mistake into a success.

As time went on, I found driving and doing shows a strain, and I disposed of the van, and relied on a friend of mine, who owned a taxi business, and he provided a taxi any time when it was required.

Of all entertainment business, the most difficult and hardest work is for an audience of children; the fees are nowhere in comparison to any other type of performance, and there is no stardom in this field of entertainment. I have been a children's entertainer for many years, and like the very few performers in this line feel that someone has to entertain them. A performance for children generally lasts one hour, whether it is Punch and Judy, magic, ventriloquism or of any other type. They will tear a performer to pieces if he is not experienced enough to deal with them; on the other hand, if a performer is good and knows his stuff, they are the most appreciative audience of all.

Before accepting an engagement for a children's show, it is necessary to know the ages of the children, so that the programme can be arranged accordingly. Some of the children are so young, even babies, that a performer has almost to play with them, and if one of them begins to cry either the mother must pacify it or take it away. On one occasion the lady responsible to pay me my fee bunged a child in my arms, and said, 'I will settle your fee. You don't mind holding the baby till I get it?'

The child had been eating some sticky sweets, its sticky hands were all over my face, and my dress shirt also came in for some attention, so you can judge for yourself what a children's entertainer has to contend with.

For many years I was a private entertainer prepared to work under any conditions, for adults or children. With children, a programme has to be arranged to suit all ages, maybe in a field, schoolroom, hall or in a private house. It is necessary to have the audience in front of you, since some tricks need a background, and if you are surrounded by the audience this sort of trick must be replaced by something which does not need a background.

I used to do a nine- or ten-minute magic act, and if you exceeded that time, you never got a return date; in fact sometimes a long stick with a crook handle used to emerge from the wings, which was conveniently placed around your neck and you were hauled off – they had some tough methods in the old days! I used to open my act with a quick spectacular trick with silk handkerchiefs, something with colour. This got the audience interested from the start, and I then proceeded with various other items, until the grand finale of a spectacular trick, probably with a production of flags, a round of applause and 'Curtain'. With children's shows I still work on those lines. You must have a good opening number to get the audience interested from the moment you come on, otherwise your show will fall flat – and a spectacular number for the finish, to get the applause you expect.

For many years a children's party came to Hayling Island; a certain hotel used to cater for them, and I was engaged to perform to them in the hotel should the weather be wet; otherwise the children were let loose to enjoy themselves in the fair, on the beach. Each year I went there, and each year it was fine weather so, without doing a show, I collected my fee and went home.

One year I said to the organizer: 'I have been engaged by you, and so far I have not done a show!'

He replied, 'I am very pleased to have you here. You are the finest assurance of fine weather!' Strange to relate I never did do a performance when the weather was not fine.

On one occasion I was engaged at a very old house at Southbourne in Hampshire. The gentleman who engaged me said, 'I don't want the children to see you, it's a surprise for them, if I open the window of the room, perhaps you can get in that way.' My assistant and I clambered through with the props, but the ceiling was the lowest I had ever seen, a middle height man could easily touch it with his hand. Although the Punch and Judy Show is made in two sections for lowering, this was beyond everything.

The gentleman looked in and, seeing my difficulty, produced hammer, wire, nails, pincers and many more things he thought useful. I took the top section as low as the ceiling would permit, and wired and roped it to the lower section. Owing to the lowness of the show, I had to adopt a crouching position, so as not to show my head and shoulders. It was one of the most uncomfortable shows I ever did, and I was certainly on my knees when I had finished.

I had several engagements booked up one year, when I became ill with a nervous complaint. I couldn't very well cancel them, so I struggled through the shows as well as I could, then I took a complete rest from show business. The old adage, 'Not so young as I used to be', came into force.

After I had recovered from this, I did not take such an active part in the show line, although I am just as nimble with my fingers and can perform the Punch and Judy Show as before, but now only accept local engagements.

I often puzzle customers in the bar with the various tricks and even now I am continually asked to do the Ascot Gold Cup. On some occasions, especially at Christmas, I have been requested by the customers to do the Punch and Judy Show for them, so I have rigged the old show up in the room, and they have enjoyed it, as though they were children. Before I conclude my experiences as a showman I should like to recall some of the great illusionists and artists in kindred lines of bygone days.

I remember as a boy the Great Lafayette in the Sculptors Dream, in which he built the statue of a woman, which came to life. It is said of him that he noticed the drummer of the orchestra so resembled himself that he asked him if he would like to join his company; the drummer did, and Lafayette worked some wonderful illusions using the drummer as a double. Lafayette was very fond of animals, and in trying to save his horse from a fire in a theatre at Edinburgh, both he and the ex-drummer perished; on recovering the bodies it was difficult to distinguish one from the other.

Buatice De Kolta was another illusionist, with his expanding dice, and the first performer, as far as I know, to vanish a bird-cage without any sort of covering.

The Great Blondin, who crossed the Niagara Falls on a tight rope, with a man in a wheel-barrow.

Then there was Maskelyne, the illusionist, who exposed the mysteries of the Davenport Brothers, spiritualistic quacks. Afterwards it became Maskelyne and Cook and then Maskelyne and Devante of St George's Hall, London.

David Devante was considered the King of Magicians, a fine performer both with sleight-of-hand and illusions, and some of his mysteries died with him.

Servais Le Roy, who cremated a woman on a high pedestal and produced her elsewhere.

Paul Cinquevalli, the great juggler – one of his main items was to throw a cannon ball into the air and catch it on the back of his neck.

The great Carl Hertz, illusionist, who vanished a bird-cage and bird between his hands. He had a court case, as the R.S.P.C.A. said he must in some ways hurt the bird. Carl Hertz had to reveal the trick in court to prove that the bird was not injured in any way, and won the day.

Harry Houdini, the great escapologist; one of his publicity stunts was being buried alive in a box for about an hour, and on being dug up was as fresh as a daisy; another stunt was being manacled, put into a sack, nailed in a box and thrown into the water, from which he escaped within seconds.

No prison in the world could hold him; at one prison he was locked in a cell, and within a short time changed all the prisoners around.

One thing had Harry Houdini puzzled for a while; he was manacled and presumably locked in a cell. He soon released himself from the handcuffs and chains and was tackling the door of the cell, and picking the lock, but it seemed adamant. He gave the door a tug and it opened, it had been purposely left unlocked. I believe Harry Houdini died of hardening of the arteries. Now I come to the Great Chinese illusionist, Chung Ling Soo, who presented a show of Oriental splendour, Chinese to the very letter – but Chung Ling Soo was a Scot. He visited China, studied their ways and mannerisms and, with a superb make-up, one would not know that he was not a Chinaman. After a grand opening, Chung Ling Soo never spoke a word, but kept an immobile facial expression while his attendants spoke for him in broken English. At a clap of his hands everything worked with clockwork precision; he was a marvellous performer in this style of magic. The story about him was that he was not the original Chung Ling Soo; the original had been a real Chinaman, but the Scot saw great possibilities of a big Chinese show; so successful was he, that the original Chung Ling Soo was forced to change his name to Chung Ling Foo. Chung Ling Soo was shot dead at a theatre in London, by his assistant, whilst doing the bullet trick. I have often wondered whether this was accidental or otherwise.

About the same time 'The Great Carmo' was running a big magical show. Originally, 'Carmo' was a circus worker and weight-lifter. But he produced a big stage show of magic and one of his illusions was to enter the lion's cage, so that instantly he and the lion disappeared and Carmo appeared from the side of the stage on a white horse.

Every Christmas he had a return date at the Hippodrome, Portsmouth. On the stage he had a huge Christmas tree loaded with presents for the children, which his attendants distributed. Carmo decided to return to circus life, but he had a run of bad luck. Both his big tops were destroyed, one by very rough weather, and one by fire. After this he returned to the stage. The last time I saw Carmo was with E.N.S.A.; he was then eighty years old.

Oswald Williams, another illusionist, had made a simple trick of tearing a strip of paper, and restoring it into a first-class illusion by his presentation, and Kalanag, a German illusionist, one of whose features was vanishing a lighted oil lamp under a cloth, whilst amongst the audience.

The 'Great Levante' was an Australian performer. One of his illusions was to have his lady assistant locked in a trunk placed inside a cabinet. Levante took his place in the cabinet and, with just his head protruding from the curtain, in less than three seconds the lady appeared and Levante was found locked in the trunk.

One performer of note I forgot and that was Arnald de Biere. Apart from his illusions, he made a speciality of the appearing and disappearing egg in a bag. There are many more performers in the art of magic too numerous to mention, but I have described the leading performers of yesterday.

My task is now over, so Cheerio.